"God's Outreach Plan: Marketing the Church in Modern Times

DR. MANFRED GOBAI, PH.D.

Published by:

K D Publishing

Copyright Page

"God's Outreach Plan: Marketing the Church in Modern Times"
Copyright © 2024 by Dr. Manfred Gobai, Ph.D.

All rights reserved.

No part of this publication may be reproduced, distributed, or transmitted in any form or by any means, including photocopying, recording, or other electronic or mechanical methods, without the prior written permission of the author, except in the case of brief quotations embodied in critical reviews and specific other noncommercial uses permitted by copyright law.

For permission requests, contact the author directly through the publisher platform.

Published by (KDP), Seattle, Washington.

ISBN: 9798304469418
Imprint: Independently published

Contents

Dedication

This book is dedicated to all who tirelessly serve in ministry, pouring their hearts and souls into reaching others with the transformative love of Christ. To pastors, church leaders, marketing teams, volunteers, and every person who works to make a difference in their community, your dedication inspires us, and this work is a testament to your unwavering commitment. May this be a tool to equip your efforts and reinforce your determination to share the Gospel in today's ever-changing world. This is for the unsung heroes, the quiet servants, the tireless workers who faithfully serve God's kingdom often behind the scenes, making an immeasurable difference. Your faith and perseverance stand as beacons of hope, and this book is the small token of our contributions to the body of Christ in support of your invaluable effort.

We would like to dedicate this work to all those nameless individuals whose lives were touched by the grace and love of God, teaching us a lesson on faith and how the Gospel message can bring about a metamorphosis. We pray that this book will equip and encourage you to share that life-changing power with others, spreading God's Kingdom one heart at a time. To those who have felt the weight of responsibility, the uncertainty of the path, and the seemingly impossible challenges of ministry, this book is dedicated in the hope that it offers comfort, guidance, and renewed purpose. May it be a source of strength and encouragement on your journey in faith, reminding you always that God's love and guidance are with you.

Preface

In a world saturated with messages, it's easy for the church's voice to be lost in the noise. This book, "God's Outreach Plan: Marketing the Church in Modern Times," is not about creating flashy campaigns or chasing fleeting trends. It's about reclaiming the essence of Christian outreach and sharing the Gospel authentically and effectively. We believe that effective church marketing is rooted in prayer, guided by God's Word, and fueled by a deep commitment to His love and truth. This isn't a manual for manipulating numbers or boosting attendance; it's a guide for cultivating genuine connections and fostering spiritual growth within communities. It's about measuring success not by likes and shares but by transforming lives and strengthening faith. Inside these pages, you will discover practical strategies for reaching people where they are, leveraging both traditional and digital platforms to share the transformative power of Christ. We delve into the importance of defining your church's unique message, understanding your target audience, and creating engaging content that reflects God's character. We encourage a shift from focusing solely on measurable metrics to embracing the more profound, meaningful impact of connecting hearts with the love of Christ. The journey of faith is not always easy; navigating the modern communication landscape requires wisdom, discernment, and reliance on the Holy Spirit's guidance. We hope this book equips you with the tools and inspiration to embark on this journey with confidence and grace, knowing that God's presence and power are your greatest assets. We've incorporated real-world examples, practical checklists, and reflective questions designed to challenge, inspire, and empower you to create a legacy of faith and service.

Introduction

God called the church to reach out to the lost and share with them the Good News of Salvation, and the ways of outreach should not stand in contrast to a rapidly changing world. "God's Outreach Plan: Marketing the Church in Modern Times" responds to this challenge: a call to innovative strategy juxtaposed against steadfast commitment to God's truth. This is not a book about appropriating secular marketing techniques and applying them to the church. It's about bringing faith and marketing together in such a way that honors God's character and reflects His love. We recognize the importance of effective communication, but we would counter that true outreach is an expression of a deeper interest in connecting with people at their spiritual point of need. It's about building relationships, community, and leading people closer to Christ. You'll find, throughout this book, principles rooted in scripture and practical strategies you can immediately put into practice. I explore defining your church's unique message, identifying your ideal audience, and choosing the proper communication channels to share the Gospel effectively. I delve into the use of digital platforms while emphasizing the importance of community engagement and the power of storytelling. Crucially, I challenge the traditional focus on superficial metrics, advocating for a shift towards measuring success by the transformative impact on individuals and communities. I believe that actual growth is reflected in lives changed, faith strengthened, and disciples made. This book is designed to be a resource for pastors, church leaders, marketing teams, and anyone involved in spreading the Gospel. I encourage you to approach each chapter with prayerful reflection, allowing the Holy Spirit to guide you as you discern how to apply these principles to your context. I hope this book will inspire and enlighten you to formulate an effective, long-lasting outreach plan that brings glory to God and changes lives. May the journey be in faith, in cooperation, and in tireless commitment to spreading the love of Christ.

Chapter 1

Understanding God's Mandate for Outreach

The Biblical Basis for Church Marketing

The call to share the Gospel is inherent in the fabric of scripture, forming the very bedrock of Christian faith and practice. From the Great Commission in Matthew 28:18-20, where Jesus instructs his disciples to "go and make disciples of all nations," to the many parables and teachings that insist on the need to spread the good news, the Bible offers a strong theological basis for outreach and, by extension, church marketing. Understanding this biblical basis is crucial in developing practical and authentic marketing strategies that are not merely promotional but deeply rooted in faith and mission.

The Great Commission itself provides a strong starting point. It is not a suggestion but a direct command from the resurrected Christ. "go" and "make disciples" are active verbs, demanding action and engagement. This active engagement necessitates strategic planning and execution, which is a concept not dissimilar to modern marketing strategies. The phrase "all nations" highlights the global scope of this mission, demanding an approach that transcends geographical boundaries and cultural differences. This means leveraging diverse communication channels to reach an international audience in today's interconnected world.

The book of Acts provides compelling examples of early Christians engaging in outreach. Through the Holy Spirit, the apostles proclaimed the Gospel in the public square, using every available method to reach different audiences. It wasn't just about delivering a message; it was about showing God's love through serving, healing, and having compassion. This integrated approach and practical demonstration remain critical to effective church marketing. It is more than assembling people in church; it involves building relationships, nurturing the community towards Christ's values, and making them alive in their day-to-day lives.

Jesus' parables are full of dynamic storylines and identifiable characters. These stories have provided great spiritual truths relevant to diverse audiences at all levels. For example, the parable of the Sower illustrates the challenges and rewards of sharing the Gospel, highlighting the importance of preparing the ground (connecting with people's needs) and persevering despite obstacles. These parables offer valuable lessons for contemporary church marketers, reminding us that effective communication requires understanding our audience, tailoring our message to their needs, and patiently nurturing relationships.

While the epistles of Paul are often theological, numerous passages emphasize the transforming power of spreading the Gospel. The tireless missionary journeys of Paul, recorded in Acts, are testimony to his commitment to reach new communities and establish churches. His letters are theological treatises and strategic communications designed to address specific needs and challenges within the early Christian communities he established. The pastoral epistles include 1

Timothy and Titus. These provide practical insight into church leadership and community engagement and can be valuable for those leading their churches' outreach efforts. That will include the selection of leaders, the resolution of conflicts, and the fostering of unity and purpose. These are key elements in effective church marketing.

The Psalms and Proverbs hold much spiritual insight that might give a backbone to our marketing strategies. The Psalms express the full range of human emotions, acknowledging joy and sorrow, faith and doubt. This propensity is a powerful ingredient in effective communication. A transparent and vulnerable approach, reflective of the empathy and understanding shown through the Psalms, can better relate and thus connect with audiences who might be more resistant or cynical. In the same light, wisdom literature such as the Book of Proverbs conveys practical advice about communications, relationships, and leadership. Emphasis on integrity, honesty, and wisdom aligns directly with authentic and ethical church marketing principles.

We see one reoccurring theme throughout scripture: God's initiative in reaching humanity. From the creation narrative to the incarnation of Christ, God actively pursued a relationship with his people. This should be the cornerstone of our marketing efforts. We are not waiting for people to come to us; we are going out to them, proclaiming the good news of God's love and grace. Such an active reaching out calls for creativity and innovation. For example, sharing social media testimony, engaging in interactive online Bible studies, and participating in community service events are great opportunities to express ourselves with our technological and cultural contexts in mind. However, such strategies must always be deeply anchored in our faith's insight and authentic communication. The Bible teaches us the importance of love, compassion, and service as integral to our outreach. The ministry of Jesus illustrates this succinctly. He reached out to the marginalized, the outcast, and the forgotten. He showed God's love through healing, compassion, and forgiveness. This model of outreach needs to shape our marketing efforts. It's not just about the numbers; it's about making a tangible difference in people's lives. This may mean partnering with local charities, offering support to those in need, or simply listening to those struggling.

The biblical call to outreach is not about numbers but about life transformation. While metrics can be beneficial for information, they should not be the measure of success. The proper measure of successful church marketing is the number of transformed lives, strengthened faith, and growing God's kingdom. This requires a shift in perspective, moving from solely numerical growth to a focus on discipleship, spiritual formation, and genuine community engagement.

The Bible has much to say about God's mandate for outreach and how it applies to the modern church marketing effort. As we root our strategies in the Scripture, the efforts will be practical yet meaningful and genuinely reflective of God's character and love. The challenge for today's churches is not to change with the modern landscape but to use it to fulfill the Great Commission, using the wisdom of scripture and the power of the Holy Spirit to reach a world in desperate need of God's grace. This is a call to action, a call to creativity, and a call to prayerful dependence on the Holy Spirit's guidance as we do the crucial work of sharing the Gospel in the 21st century. Shifting from Metrics to Mission

The previous section established the biblical basis for church outreach, highlighting the unwavering command to share the Gospel. However, the modern church often grapples with a significant challenge: the temptation to equate success with numerical growth, measured by easily quantifiable metrics. While attendance numbers, website visits, and social media engagement are valuable data points, they should never become the ultimate indicators of a thriving ministry. This subsection addresses the crucial shift from a metrics-driven approach to a mission-focused one, emphasizing the importance of spiritual transformation and discipleship.

We live in an age obsessed with numbers. The pressure to demonstrate tangible results, often expressed in quantifiable metrics, permeates every aspect of modern life, and the church is no exception. Church leaders, often under pressure from congregations and governing bodies, may prioritize numerical growth. A larger congregation, a higher social media following, and a packed event symbolize success, sometimes overshadowing spiritual growth and discipleship's more profound, less easily measurable aspects. This focus on vanity metrics, as they are sometimes called, can distort the church's true purpose. It can result in marketing strategies prioritizing attracting large numbers rather than cultivating genuine faith and fostering a deep relationship with God.

The problem with this approach is multifaceted. Firstly, it risks compromising the integrity of the Gospel message. Strategies designed solely to inflate numbers might employ manipulative tactics, focusing on superficial appeals rather than the transformative power of the Holy Spirit. Concentrating on attracting a large audience might lead to diluting the message, dumbing it down, or tailoring it to appeal to the lowest common denominator rather than challenging individuals to confront their sin and embrace the life-changing truth of Jesus Christ. Secondly, relentlessly pursuing numerical growth can lead to burnout among church leadership and volunteers. The constant pressure to increase numbers can become overwhelming, leading to exhaustion and disillusionment, ultimately hindering the very mission they strive to achieve.

The solution lies in a fundamental shift in perspective. Instead of focusing on vanity metrics, we must prioritize individuals' genuine spiritual transformation and the church's growth as a body of believers committed to Christ. This requires a clear understanding of what constitutes true success in God's eyes. Proper growth is not merely about increasing headcount; it's about nurturing disciples who are actively growing in their faith, engaging in meaningful worship, serving others, and sharing the Gospel with the world. It is about seeing lives transformed, relationships deepened, and communities strengthened by the power of the Holy Spirit. It is about creating disciples who, in turn, become disciple-makers.

Consider the parable of the Sower and the seed (Matthew 13:1-23). The seed represents the Gospel message; the soil represents the hearts of individuals. Jesus highlights the various types of soil—some receptive, some resistant—illustrating that not every seed will bear fruit. The focus isn't on the number of seeds sown but on the number that take root, grow, and produce a harvest. Similarly, church outreach should not be solely measured by the number of people attending a service or liking a Facebook post. The accurate measure of success lies in the number of lives transformed by the power of the Gospel, the number of disciples actively engaged in their faith, and the number of people who come to know Christ and experience his love.

How do we shift from a metrics-driven to a mission-focused approach? It begins with prayerful reflection and a renewed commitment to God's will. It involves critically examining current outreach strategies and identifying areas where the focus has shifted from spiritual transformation to mere numerical growth. This necessitates a reevaluation of what constitutes success. Instead of focusing on easily quantifiable metrics, we should develop more nuanced and holistic measures of effectiveness.

This might involve tracking qualitative data, such as the number of individuals who have made a profession of faith, the level of engagement in small groups and Bible studies, the number of people involved in serving the community, and the overall spiritual maturity of the congregation. It might also include conducting regular feedback sessions with church members to assess their spiritual growth and identify areas where support is needed. Additionally, it's vital to create a culture within the church that values discipleship and spiritual growth above all else. This requires investing in leadership training, providing opportunities for spiritual formation, and fostering a supportive community where individuals feel empowered to grow in their faith.

The transition from a metrics-driven to a mission-focused approach also requires a shift in our language. Instead of "reaching targets" or "increasing engagement," we should focus on nurturing faith, building relationships, and sharing the love of Christ. This subtle shift in language can profoundly impact the overall culture and direction of the church. It helps remind everyone that the ultimate goal is not to impress people with numbers but to touch hearts with the Gospel's transformative power.

Church leaders must clearly articulate the church's vision and mission, emphasizing the importance of spiritual growth and discipleship over mere numerical growth. This communication should be consistent and transparent, ensuring that everyone in the church understands the underlying principles guiding the ministry's outreach efforts. Regular updates and progress reports on qualitative growth will help keep the congregation informed and engaged in the mission.

We must recognize that actual growth takes time. Spiritual transformation is not a quick fix; it's a gradual process that requires patience, perseverance, and a deep reliance on the Holy Spirit. Church leaders and members alike need to cultivate a spirit of patience and trust, trusting that God is at work in the hearts and lives of individuals, even if the results are not immediately apparent. We need to remember that God's timeline is not our own. Our role is to faithfully share the Gospel, to nurture the seeds of faith, and to trust that God will bring forth the harvest in His own time and way. The focus should be on faithfulness rather than immediate, measurable results.

Shifting from metrics to mission requires fundamentally reorientating our priorities and perspectives. It transitions from a superficial, numbers-driven approach to a deep, soul-focused ministry. It necessitates a reassessment of success, replacing easily quantifiable metrics with more holistic and meaningful measures of spiritual growth and discipleship. By embracing this shift, we can move away from the pressures of vanity metrics and focus on the true purpose of the church: to glorify God and make disciples of all nations. This journey demands courage, faith, and a commitment to prioritize genuine spiritual transformation above all else to measure success not by the numbers but by the lives transformed by the power of the Gospel. The challenge is to grow the church and the kingdom of God, one transformed life at a time.

God's Character as the Foundation of Outreach

Our understanding of God's mandate for outreach must be deeply rooted in the very character of God Himself. It is insufficient to proclaim the Gospel; we must live it in every aspect of our endeavor to reach out. The transactional approach to evangelism, primarily individualistic in its ultimate goal of conversion, must be relational, reflecting God's love, compassion, and truth. Authentic outreach is born out of a deep-seated desire to reach people on a human level, understand their needs and struggles, and present the transformative power of Christ as a source of hope and healing.

The Bible presents God as a God of unwavering love. His love is not conditional; it's not earned or deserved. It's a freely given gift poured out upon a fallen humanity. 1 John 4:8 says, "Whoever does not love does not know God, because God is love." This truth needs to be the foundation of our marketing strategy. Our outreach materials, social media presence, and community engagement should exude this unconditional love. We should seek to communicate in empathetic, understanding, and non-judgmental messages. This does not mean compromising the truth of the Gospel but articulating it with grace and compassion, realizing the brokenness inherent in the human condition.

Imagine the impact of a social media campaign focused on solutions to societal ills rather than criticizing them. Instead of condemning behaviors, we could offer resources for people struggling with addiction, depression, or loneliness. We can also collaborate with local organizations that provide these services, give voice to them, and create a network of care. This approach is very much in line with the heart of God, who consistently demonstrates His love in concrete ways. This is more convincing than mere condemnation and builds trust, allowing the Gospel to fall on the fertile ground of compassion.

His truth is unwavering: God is not a God of deception or falsehood. His word is truth, and His promises are sure. It is this commitment to truth that must constitute the foundation of our efforts at outreach. We must ensure all our communications are truthful, clear, and transparent. We should not sensationalize, exaggerate, or manipulate in any way. The integrity of our message is critical. People are discerning; they can recognize authenticity from artifice. A marketing strategy based on truth and transparency engenders trust, and good relationships can be built where there is trust.

Imagine a website for your church that looks great but is also user-friendly and informative. It would have easily accessible answers to frequently asked questions, honest responses to people's doubts and questions, and clear pathways to get involved with the church community. This would express God's love for truth and transparency—a place where people can feel secure and wanted. This would be much more effective than putting slick images with catchy slogans on some poorly organized websites.

God is also faithful. He keeps His promises, and His love endures for generations. This faithfulness to God should be reflected in our outreach strategies. We must be consistent in our work, showing our reliability and perseverance. We must follow through on what we say we will do and invest in long-term relationships with those we reach. This ongoing commitment fosters trust and encourages deeper engagement.

A long-term outreach project could involve mentoring underprivileged youth, regularly supporting needy families, or volunteering at a local homeless shelter. These acts of service, done consistently over time, speak volumes to God's character and allow people to see and experience the Gospel in practical and tangible ways. When people see the message being lived out in real life through consistent faithfulness by the church community, they are more apt to believe it.

But besides love, the truth, and faithfulness, God is described as holy and just. As much as our outreach should be wrapped in love and compassion, we must remember we are serving a sacred God who calls us to live righteous lives. That does not mean being judgmental or condemnatory; instead, we mustn't water down the truth of the Gospel. We must boldly proclaim God's word, address social injustices, and call for repentance.

This calls for a careful approach. For instance, our efforts should be solution-oriented in advocating for social justice, not merely condemning those who take a different view. This may involve partnering with organizations to address poverty, racism, or human trafficking and highlighting their work in our outreach campaigns. This approach emulates God's justice and mercy and shows the Gospel's transformative power in real-life problems.

Yet, even as we embrace this calling to be lowly and serve, our God can do great deeds. That, in itself, ought to give our outreach efforts the grounds for confidence and boldness. We are to show no reservation in sharing the Gospel but trust in God's might as He moves in our lives.

It is not arrogant; instead, it's the faith and realization of God's working power and the trust that change will happen through that process. This might mean stepping out of our comfort zones to share our faith in unlikely places or praying for boldness to engage in religious conversations with friends and family members with different perspectives. This confidence springs from our reliance on God's strength and our conviction that the Gospel is the good news that the world desperately needs.

Effective church outreach isn't about numbers or strategies but about reflecting the very character of God in every aspect of our ministry. As God's love, truth, faithfulness, justice, and power begin to be the foundation we market, effective connections with people can be made, trust can be built, and the Gospel's transformative power can be shared profoundly and authentically. It is a journey that requires humility, prayer, and an ongoing striving to reflect the image of God in all we do. It's about realizing that the size of our church does not define success, but by hearts transformed and the growth of God's Kingdom-one life, one family, one community at a time. Such change is a testament to the work of God's grace and power, not our prowess in marketing. Let us at all times remember to glory God in any growth or success.

Overcoming Barriers to Authentic Outreach

Overcoming the ingrained hesitations and practical challenges of embracing a faith-based marketing approach requires a multifaceted strategy. Many churches, deeply rooted in tradition and often operating on limited resources, are hesitant to adopt modern marketing techniques. This resistance stems from various sources, and addressing it requires understanding the root causes and offering practical, faith-based solutions.

One significant barrier is the fear of misrepresenting the Gospel. Pastors and church leaders often fear marketing strategies will make their ministry tactics manipulative or profane the message itself. This fear is somewhat understandable, given the misinterpretation of the call to "go and make disciples" (Matthew 28:19). What needs to be done is to change the paradigm from one of "selling" the Gospel to "sharing" it. In this context, marketing is to be the method of facilitating connection and creating meaningful conversations, not a tool of coercion. The focus must stay on authentically communicating the transformative power of Christ's love and grace rather than numerical growth at any cost. This requires excellent consideration in messaging, platforms used, and tone. Authenticity demands transparency, admitting vulnerabilities, and understanding that the church community is on a faith journey.

Another common barrier involves resistance to change. Many churches cling to traditional ways of outreach, often with suspicion toward new methods. This resistance usually comes from a need to be educated on how modern marketing tools can support, not replace, long-established practices. It is essential to frame the adoption of new strategies not as a rejection of the past but as an evolution- a way to reach a broader audience in a rapidly changing world. Workshops, training sessions, and mentorship programs can bridge the gap between tradition and innovation. Showing the success of faith-based marketing in other churches and showing case studies and testimonials will also help alleviate concerns and build confidence.

Another major challenge is resource limitations, such as financial and human. Many churches have to live on a shoestring budget without the personnel to manage complicated marketing campaigns. This means that effective outreach is possible through creative, cost-effective strategies that use free or low-cost digital platforms, volunteers' skills, and concentrate on community partnerships. This may be by reaching out to the community using other means besides expensive print advertising: asking local businesses to hand out flyers or simply posting their message using free social media. Strong volunteer recruitment and training can compensate for the personnel constraints, making church members agents of contribution with unique talents and skills. Furthermore, grants or crowdfunding may be available to lighten some financial burdens. What matters is how resources available are used creatively to attest to resourcefulness and faith in God's provision.

The seeming lack of expertise in marketing and digital technologies is a big hurdle. Most church leaders are made to feel incapable of using social media, website design, or data analysis effectively. This perceived inability has often led to a no-action or ineffective strategy for the church. To this effect, churches should be interested in training and mentorship programs. Again, engaging marketing professionals who understand and respect a church's particular needs and vision is beneficial. Most marketing pros will volunteer to work gratis or at significantly reduced rates for faith-based entities. This approach brings valuable skill into the ministry while remaining sensitive to theological integrity and church vision. Similarly, people with the appropriate abilities, actual or potential, are identified and released within the congregation. This capacity building may be significantly complemented by mentoring programs in which experienced people guide the newcomers. Another more subtle but formidable barrier is internal division within the church itself. There are disagreements over how to market, the appropriateness of specific methods, and sometimes a lack of consensus, even among the church leadership. This can cause delays in progress and a general atmosphere of negativity. It requires open and honest dialogue based on mutual respect and a shared vision. It is up to the leadership to provide a facilitating atmosphere where different opinions can be heard and constructive conversations are entertained. Transparency in decision-making processes helps ensure one feels heard and involved. A consensus on the general marketing objectives of the church and some agreed-upon ways of measurement for success is critical in building unity and support. Here, prayer and spiritual discernment should form part of the process so that the church is directed toward strategies that align with God's will and the community's particular needs.

Beyond these practical challenges, deeper theological considerations influence a church's approach to outreach. Some may believe that relying on marketing strategies diminishes the role of the Holy Spirit in evangelism. However, a balanced perspective recognizes God's use of varied tools and methods to reach individuals; marketing can be seen as an instrument through which God does His big plan. The emphasis goes on prayer, seeking the guidance of God, and believing in the work of the Holy Spirit within the methods chosen. It is not to replace spiritual practices but to complement their effectiveness in strategically communicating the church's message to a larger group. There is a great temptation to fall into measuring success merely by quantifiable metrics: website traffic, social media engagement, and attendance numbers. This will create a false understanding of actual growth. While data analysis is functional, it should always include the qualitative aspects of ministry: transformed lives, strengthened faith, and deeper relationships within the community. Authentic outreach prioritizes building genuine connections, offering genuine support, and nurturing spiritual growth. This requires a shift in perspective from focusing on numbers to concentrating on people. In contrast, regular prayer, reflection, and feedback mechanisms can give a more accurate account of the outreach efforts concerning these qualitative measures. The goal is to draw large crowds rather than to build a dynamic, caring community of faith.

It takes an active and multi-faceted effort to break through barriers that hinder genuine outreach. Addressing fears, embracing change, using resources efficiently, building expertise, promoting unity, and maintaining a balanced theological perspective will help formulate a faith-based marketing strategy that shows God's love and enables the church to communicate the Gospel in today's world effectively. By approaching outreach with humility, in prayer, and with deep devotion to God's leading, churches can break down these barriers and embrace the transformative power of authentic, faith-based marketing. The journey may be difficult, but the rewards are immeasurable: God's Kingdom grows, and lives are changed.

Prayer and Guidance in Strategic Planning

Prayer It is not a supplementary activity to be tacked onto the end of our strategic planning sessions but the very bedrock upon which our whole outreach strategy must be based. Without a consistent, vibrant prayer life threaded through every aspect of our marketing efforts, we risk building our house on sand, exposed to the stormy weather of doubt, distraction, and ineffectiveness. This isn't about magical thinking, hoping for divine intervention to bypass hard work. Instead, it's about seeking God's wisdom, discerning His will, and aligning our human efforts with His holy purposes.

The process begins before we start brainstorming specific campaigns or choosing marketing channels. Before we consider website design or social media strategies, we must seek God's guidance on the overall direction of our outreach. This would involve regular, specific prayer times, maybe as a church leadership team seeking His will for our congregation. We must ask ourselves: What needs exist within our community that we are uniquely positioned to address? What is the spiritual hunger that God is prompting us to fill? What gifts and talents has He given to our church body that we can leverage for effective outreach? These are not questions to be answered through market research alone; they require spiritual discernment, guided by prayer and careful listening to the Holy Spirit.

Once we have a clearer understanding of God's direction, prayer continues to be integral throughout the planning phase. As we brainstorm ideas, we should bring each concept before God, seeking His confirmation or correction. We may consider a new community event, a revamped website, or a targeted social media campaign. Of course, each of these initiatives deserves prayerful consideration. We might pray, "Lord, is this the right path? Will this strategy truly honor You and effectively reach those You desire to touch?" We should not fear asking hard questions, admitting our limitations, and trusting His wisdom to lead us to the best course of action.

Practicing prayer in this phase might involve incorporating dedicated prayer times into team meetings. Before discussing specific marketing tactics, begin with prayer, asking for clarity, wisdom, and unity. After brainstorming, dedicate time to prayerfully considering the ideas generated. This process involves more than simply listing ideas; it consists of discerning which ideas best align with God's character, our church's mission, and the needs of our community. This requires a discerning heart, sensitive to the promptings of the Holy Spirit.

Beyond the initial planning stages, prayer must permeate the execution of our strategies. As we develop our marketing materials, whether writing website copy, designing social media graphics, or preparing event programs, we should pray for God's blessing on these efforts. We can pray for clarity of message, that the words would penetrate hearts, and the visuals clearly and effectively depict God's love and truth. This is not simply a matter of producing top-of-the-line marketing materials but a way of saturating these with spiritual power and asking God to make them instruments of His grace.

For example, this could be when a church starts a new outreach to young people. The planning team comprised passionate youth leaders and experienced church members who spent weeks brainstorming. They prayed extensively, seeking God's guidance on the program's format, activities, and target audience. Through prayer, they recognized a need within their community for a safe and supportive space for teenagers struggling with identity and purpose. They had initially planned on purely a sports-based program but later designed one based on mentorship, Bible study, and creative arts. The prayerful discernment led them to an approach that would be much more effective and relevant.

Another critical point of prayer in our strategies involves the evaluation phase of our marketing. We may use such metrics as website traffic or social media engagement, but the accurate measure of success should be based on spiritual impact. How many lives have been touched? How many hearts have been drawn closer to Christ? How has our outreach strengthened our church community and its relationship with God? These are questions that require prayerful reflection. We must ask God to reveal the fruits of our visible and hidden labor to discern what aspects of our strategy were compelling and where improvements are needed.

Maybe that well-thought-out social media campaign did not quite get the high engagement we had wished for. We should not simply dismiss it as a failure but look at the results prayerfully. Was the message received? Were the channels proper for our target audience? Did we give God time to act through our actions? Prayerful self-reflection can bring honest insights that will shape future strategies. This constant cycle of planning, execution, and evaluation, informed at each stage by prayer, helps to ensure that our marketing efforts align with God's purposes.

A culture of prayer must be developed within the whole church, not just the marketing team. Encourage regular prayer regarding the success of outreach efforts. This can happen through dedicated prayer times during church services, small group meetings, or online prayer requests. Such prayer creates a strong sense of unity and shared purpose in the entire church body behind the success of the outreach, thereby enhancing the effectiveness of all marketing strategies. This congregational prayer further anchors the outreach spiritually and cements its relationship to God's work.

Let it be noted that prayer is not an escape route from hard work and strenuous planning. It does not spell a magic formula for instant success. Instead, it is an integral part of the holistic marketing strategy, offering direction, insight, and judgment. It combines our human effort with God's will so that the outreach is compelling, steeped in faith, and led by the Holy Spirit. The real test of our marketing effort will be in the actual metrics, the transformation in the people, and the growth in God's Kingdom. This requires consistent dedication to prayer, a willingness to listen to God's voice, and trust that He is unchangingly guiding us. In substance, prayer provides the lifeblood to make one's outreach strategy relevant, effective, and genuinely God-honoring. Otherwise, regardless of our efforts, with the best intentions, we often end up futile. With it, we tap into an unlimited source of wisdom, power, and guidance to effectively share the Gospel and build God's Kingdom in the world.

Chapter 2

Defining Your Church's Unique Message

Discovering Your Church Core Values

Core values are not just some introspective processes within a church; they form the foundation for effective communication and outreach. It is about understanding the very core of your congregation, what sets them apart, and what gives the base for its actions and beliefs. This process is essential because it will determine the shaping of your message to current members and the greater community. Well-defined core values become a filter, so everything they do to market or get their name out is done genuinely in a manner that feels appropriate and consistent with their spiritual mission.

The discovery process involves a very active engagement process within the church. This is not to be done by a chosen few; this is intended as an effort born from and representative of your congregation's collective wisdom and experiences. Consider holding facilitated discussions, divided into smaller groups based on age, ministries, or other relevant demographic factors. These discussions should be carefully guided to avoid getting bogged down in tangential debates. The goal is to identify the fundamental beliefs and practices that define your church's identity. Questions to consider during these discussions might include:

What are the non-negotiable beliefs that shape our faith and practice? These might include theological positions on salvation, the nature of God, the role of the Bible, etc. Be specific; general statements are insufficient.

What is unique about the culture of our church? Would it be the vibrancy in worship, an emphasis on social justice, the community outreach, the welcoming environment, or anything else? Identify those things that make your church different from others.

What are the guiding principles in our interactions with one another and the greater community? Some may be love, compassion, forgiveness, service, justice, integrity, and humility. How is this expressed in the ongoing life of the church?

What are some of the milestones in our church's history that reveal our core identity? Reflecting on significant events and moments of God's work within your congregation can illuminate the underlying values that have shaped its trajectory.

What commonly held values inspire and motivate our people? Through individual testimonies and collective experiences, listen for some common themes and sentiments:

Approach these conversations in prayer and humility. Ask God to direct you as you consider them, taking great care that the Holy Spirit leads the process. The goal is not to generate an inflexible list of dos and don'ts but to discover which convictions center your church and supply the foundation upon which all other activities emanate.

When the discussions are done, it's time to synthesize the findings. Collate the input from all groups, looking for recurring themes and commonalities. Avoid merely listing every suggestion that arose; instead, strive to identify the overarching values that encapsulate the essence of your church's identity. This may lead to a list of 5-7 core values, concisely stated and easily understood by all members.

For example, one church might identify its core values as Biblical Truth, Loving Community, Transformational Worship, Compassionate Service, and Global Mission. Another might prioritize Grace, Faith, Fellowship, Discipleship, and Evangelism. The specific values will vary depending on your church's unique character and history. What is essential is that the values selected genuinely represent your congregation's beliefs and practices.

Once the core values have been identified, a crucial step is practical communication within the church. This means more than printing it out on the bulletin or putting it on a website. It needs to penetrate the church's daily life and many activities. Consider creating an infographic or a short video about your core values. These can be used publicly within the church facility, across social media platforms, and in volunteer training documents.

Revisit and reflect on your core values from time to time. Your church will continue growing and changing, which will undoubtedly bring about changed perspectives and priorities. Reaffirming and adjusting the wording, or even adding new values, is what keeps core values current and in step with your congregation's ever-changing reality.

Discovering your church's core values is not a one-time activity but a journey of self-discovery and refinement. This is a continued process of prayerful reflection, communal dialogue, and commitment to an authentic witness of life. By planting your church's marketing and outreach into these core values, you will ensure a genuine and consistent message is deeply rooted in the heart of faith. It's about ensuring that every action and message accurately reflects the values that define your church's identity and mission. This authentic approach will resonate more deeply with your existing congregation and attract those in your community searching for a place of genuine faith and spiritual growth.

To ensure the process is inclusive and avoids inadvertently marginalizing voices within the church, consider implementing these additional steps:

- Diverse Representation: The groups involved should cover all the demographics within your church, from all ages, ethnicities, and socio-economic backgrounds to differences in church involvement. This assures comprehensive insight into the collected values.

- Anonymous Feedback Mechanisms: Provide channels through which people can give anonymous feedback for fear of judgment or retaliation. This may include online surveys or suggestion boxes where people can confidentially provide their views.

- Multiple Channels of Communication: Employ multiple channels to solicit input. Do not restrict yourself to face-to-face meetings. Surveys, online forums, or casual discussions can gather more diverse perspectives.

- Professional Facilitation: Consider engaging a trained facilitator to lead the discussion groups. A neutral third party can help ensure productive, unbiased conversations, preventing dominant personalities from overshadowing quieter voices.

- Transparency and Accountability: Communicate the process and findings transparently with the congregation. Explain how the input received shaped the final set of core values. This communicates accountability and fosters trust among members.

You will establish in your church a sound core of values that captures the essence of your church's identity and may act as a guide to outreach in years to come. Remember, this isn't some marketing ploy but is representative of your spiritual journey together as a body led by the love and grace of God. The purpose was to create a consistent and dynamic community through fundamental shared values and devotion to the service of God and others. This brutal introspection and open communication strengthen your church from within and undergirds the foundation by which it can be more articulate and effective in its involvement with the larger community. In every respect, the resulting clarity and focus within your church's ministry contribute to deeper relationships and a sense of purpose. Identifying your core values is a form of worship, a profession of faith, and the path to better, more impactful ministry.

Crafting a Compelling Narrative

After establishing clear core values, the next most important thing in creating a strong church message is to weave those core values into the story that will deeply connect with your audience. This is more than a list of services or an announcement of events; it's a declaration of the heartbeat of your church and a description of how faith changes lives. Think of it as storytelling but on a heavenly mission. Your story needs to capture the identity of your community, history, mission, and vision for tomorrow, with how the love of Christ impacts individual lives and greater society.

This must be an attractive story that gives key answers to the visitor and prospective member. What makes this church different? What community needs does it seek to serve? What spiritual journey can people expect to take within your walls? The answers to such questions should be woven seamlessly into an inspiring, inviting story. It must go beyond a list of programs onto a living testament of faith's power of transformation.

Your congregation may have a rich history in a specific neighborhood or community. This can be a powerful part of your story, showing that the church has been committed to serving its people over the years. Was your church instrumental in some important community event? Was there a point of spiritual epiphany that defined the trajectory of the church today? These historical markers serve as a bridge of continuity and, in effect, legitimize your message.

History aside, there is the present to consider. What are some of your church's current ministries and outreach programs? Rather than list them, if possible, show how they have helped real people and the community. Is your youth group alive and well, serving a need in the lives of your young people? Does your church provide vital support services through a food bank, counseling, or other ways? Share specific examples of how these programs change lives and illustrate God's love in action. Use real-life stories from members who have benefited from these programs. Let their stories become the heart of your narrative, showing your ministry's tangible, positive outcomes. These personal stories are far more compelling than generic statements about your church's mission.

In addition, your narrative should portray your vision for the future of your church. Where will your community grow in the next five, ten, or twenty years? What are your aspirations for outreach, discipleship, and community engagement? Share this vision; it speaks of ambition, faith, and commitment to continued growth in service. It shows that your church is not static; it is a vibrant community with a clear purpose and a strong commitment to making positive changes in the world. This vision of the future could make the congregation attractive to the younger generation, most of whom are attracted to a church with a sense of direction and purpose.

In formulating a compelling narrative, consider your target audience. For whom are you developing the narrative? Young families? Retirees? Spiritual seekers? Knowing your target audience allows you to shape the message to meet their needs and goals. For example, an intergenerational community-centered message would resonate with families, a spiritual formation program message might appeal to individuals who yearn to dive deeper into their faith, and a community service-focused narrative may attract those seeking to make a difference in the world.

Avoid using too much theological vocabulary that may confuse those not used to church terms; instead, use precise, concise, relatable terminology that speaks directly to the heart. Use storytelling to make an emotional connection with them. Paint vivid pictures, evoke empathy and understanding with your words, and ignite hope and transformation.

Your story must be told the same across all your communication channels. It needs to be one single message on your website, in your social media posts, in your brochures, and in your sermons. This helps reinforce the overall story and create a strong brand identity for your church. This requires a strategic approach to content creation, ensuring that every piece of communication supports the overarching story and reflects the church's core values.

Another essential component in crafting a strong narrative is concisely articulating your church's USP. What sets your church apart from other churches in your area? Is it your emphasis on a specific ministry? Your style of worship? Your outreach to the community? Identifying your USP helps you differentiate your church and draws people looking for what your church offers. This USP needs to be smoothly integrated into your overall narrative, bringing out the uniqueness of your community and ministry.

Underestimating the power of visual communication: Your church website, social media profiles, and promotional materials should speak to your narrative visually. Use high-quality images and videos that capture the heart of your community and the joy of your faith. These can reinforce your message and make a lasting impression on potential visitors. Professional-looking visuals enhance your church's credibility and make it more appealing to potential members.

Then, regularly assess how well your story is working. Are folks responding to your message? Are you gaining members? Are you meeting your objectives regarding outreach and discipleship? Remember, the effectiveness of your narrative should be assessed and changed as necessary on an ongoing basis. Sometimes, just acquiring feedback from members and visitors can powerfully tell what works and what does not. This ongoing evaluation is crucial for ensuring that your church's message remains relevant, engaging, and effective in connecting with your target audience. Remember, the goal is not just to attract people but to nurture their spiritual growth and help them deepen their relationship with God. Your compelling narrative should be a beacon of hope, guidance, and transformative love. By carefully considering these elements, your church can craft a persuasive narrative that effectively communicates its unique message, attracts new members, and strengthens its community by our community's age range, socioeconomic status, and cultural background in your ongoing mission to share the Gospel with the world.

Identifying Your Ideal Audience

Coupled with establishing a captivating church story, knowing your target audience is the second most vital aspect of effective church marketing. This is more than understanding their age bracket and location; it means engaging in more profound levels of comprehension of hopes, fears, spiritual journeys, and challenges unlike any other. Such insights will make every minute element of outreach strategy purposefully drive the message across effectively and draw those longing for an association with God.

Defining your ideal audience goes beyond simple demographics. Of course, it's good to know your community's age range, socioeconomic status, and cultural background, but you need to dig deeper. What is the spiritual maturity level of your target group? Are you trying to reach those new to faith, seeking a church home for the first time? Or do you consider yourself a church invested in the spiritual maturing of longstanding believers, providing them with further discipleship and leadership development opportunities? Understanding this spectrum can help you in crafting appropriate messaging and programming.

A church reaching out to young adults might be invested in social media engagement, contemporary worship styles, and small group discussions of relevant life issues. By contrast, a church targeting an older audience would use more traditional media: print, newsletters, and more formal, lecture-oriented teaching. But this is an oversimplification. Even within these age groups, there are a variety of needs. Some young adults desire in-depth theological training, while others prefer a casual, relational approach. Similarly, older adults differ in technology use and worship preferences.

Thus, a proper process of identifying the audience cannot be one-dimensional. Make sure to research your community's needs and hopes with depth. This includes tools such as questionnaires, focus groups, and spontaneous discussions with members and possible visitors. Look at your existing congregation's demographics, then compare them with those in the surrounding area. This will present probable discrepancies and opportunities for outreach. Might your church serve underrepresented segments of your community more effectively? What are the most typical interests and needs of these segments?

You may want to utilize publicly available demographic information from such sources as the US Census Bureau or equivalent entities within your country. This can provide a larger context to add your more focused local community research. Bring this larger perspective with the more specific information you collect through interviews and surveys. For instance, you might discover that a significant portion of your community struggles financially. This understanding should inform your outreach strategies, potentially leading you to offer financial literacy classes, support groups, or other relevant services that address this specific need, demonstrating the church's concern and extending its compassion beyond purely spiritual matters.

Let's consider some practical examples. A suburban church may find through its community surveys that many potential audience feels disconnected and alone despite the high population density. Such a realization might lead to developing community outreach programs that help people connect, such as neighborhood potlucks, parenting support groups, or volunteering opportunities. The church can tailor a message to this identified need for belonging and community by depicting itself as an accepting and caring community providing spiritual nourishment, practical help, and social interaction.

Or, in a city location, the church may find a high population of single parents who have child-care difficulties. Perhaps the church could provide subsidized childcare during their worship so parents can feel free to attend the service without dealing with childcare logistics. This would speak volumes about the church's desire to serve the community's needs and make people from all walks of life feel welcome. The church can emphasize this in its literature, explicitly stating how functional and friendly it is to all.

Understanding your ideal audience extends beyond their immediate needs and into aspirations: What do they hope for? What do they dream about? What is important to them? What kind of spiritual community are they looking for? In discerning these deeper longings, you will fashion a message that speaks right to their hearts and profoundly reverberates with their individual and collective needs. This means going beyond the surface-level assessments and conversing with potential attendees through surveys and online engagement.

For example, a church may find that many of its target audience is very concerned about the environment. In response, the church may develop environmentally conscious programs, such as organizing community clean-up days, promoting sustainable practices, or advocating for environmental justice. This speaks to the target audience's values, showing a more profound commitment than providing spiritual support alone. The message from the church can focus on such initiatives, creating a common ground in caring for the community and the environment, further establishing rapport and trust.

Integrate feedback mechanisms as part of your ongoing improvement in understanding your ideal audience. Gather feedback through surveys, feedback forms, and one-on-one discussions on a routine basis. These interactions provide invaluable insights into what resonates with your audience, what needs improvement, and what additional needs you might have yet to identify initially. Analyze this feedback consistently to ensure your church's message and outreach strategies remain relevant, engaging, and effective in meeting the needs of those you strive to reach.

This process is not static; it's an ongoing journey of learning and adaptation. As your church grows and evolves, so does your understanding of the ideal audience. Regularly revisit your audience profile and reassess your strategies to ensure they align with your community's changing needs and aspirations. Constantly refining your understanding will enhance your effectiveness in communicating your church's unique message, creating a vibrant, inviting spiritual home for all. By embracing this dynamic approach, your church will be better positioned to connect those seeking a deeper relationship with God to build a vibrant and dynamic community rooted in faith and love. The key is not to approach audience identification as one task but as a continuous process: to listen, learn, and adapt to understand and serve the specific needs of those you are called to reach. The iterative process keeps your marketing strategies accurate, actually reflecting the heart of God's love and compassion.

Choosing the Right Communication Channels

Having defined your church's unique message and identified your target audience, the next important step is to select the proper communication channels. This includes a strategic mix of traditional and digital methods thoughtfully considered to extend reach and impact in your community and beyond. The key is to be on every conceivable platform and choose those that best fit your audience's preferences and your church's resources. It will be more of a shotgun approach, scattering your message across many channels, and there will not be much impact on results or resources. However, you can cultivate meaningful connections and foster a lively community with a targeted and focused approach.

Consider demographics and the digital literacy of your audience. Do they mostly dwell on Facebook, Instagram, or TikTok? Or would they prefer in-person and more traditional means, such as print media or word-of-mouth referrals? Understanding these preferences is key to effective communication. For example, a church desiring to reach younger adults may be very successful with Instagram and TikTok, with their visually engaging and short-form video content. A church with an older demographic may find more success through local newspaper ads, community bulletin boards, and direct mail campaigns. It is not to discard any but to focus on the means that best fit your demography. Traditional methods still work remarkably well in most communities today. Think about word-of-mouth referrals as proof and a reflection of the depth and relevance of your ministry. Encourage your membership to share their faith stories and invite friends and family. Many times, this personal touch counts much more than any advertisement. Printed materials, like flyers, brochures, and bulletins, have proven successful, especially when placed correctly within the community. Look toward local businesses, libraries, and community centers as ways to disperse your materials to a broader population. These partnerships also serve as excellent opportunities to know your community much deeper and build relationships for trust. Don't underestimate the power of a well-designed church website, a central hub for information about services, events, and ministries. It's a crucial tool for providing accessibility and information to a broader audience.

Digital channels offer incredible opportunities to reach a wider audience and engage with people in new and innovative ways. Social media platforms like Facebook, Instagram, Twitter, and YouTube provide avenues for sharing your church's message, announcing events, and building community. However, developing a consistent and engaging social media presence is crucial. Avoid sporadic posting and instead create a content calendar to ensure regular updates. Visual content, such as photos and videos, is particularly effective on platforms like Instagram and YouTube. Consider making short videos of your church's mission, values, and community activities. Livestream services and events where people are not physically present might be a part of this. Email marketing remains an effective way of connecting with the congregation and updating them about something or announcing other essential things. It can help improve effectiveness by building an e-mail list and segmenting this list based on different ministries or interests. However, remember that email etiquette is a significant concern, and do not spam recipients with too many emails.

Choosing the proper channels involves careful consideration of your church's resources. Different platforms require varying levels of time, effort, and financial investment. For instance, a full-scale social media strategy requires paid staff or volunteers to develop content, schedule, and interact with followers. Likewise, shooting quality videos or designing professional print pieces requires investing in cameras, software, or design services. Thus, developing a realistic budget and strategically allocating resources to ensure sustainable growth and avoid burnout is necessary. Go small with what's essential, then increase your scope as your experience, resources, and results grow. Feel free to try new things; remember to measure their results because that's how you can improve your strategy with time: track social media engagement metrics, monitor website traffic, and assess the performance of your traditional marketing activities. You will get a proper base for further optimization and maximum effectiveness of your ROI in general.

Beyond the specific platforms chosen, the content itself is paramount. The message should always be authentic, reflecting the heart of your church and its commitment to God's love. Avoid using overly promotional or manipulative language. Focus instead on sharing inspiring stories, offering hope and encouragement, and showcasing the transformative power of faith. Your communication should invite people to connect with God and experience the love of the community. Remember to tailor your message to the specific platform and audience. A short, visually engaging video on Instagram might be less effective on a church website, where longer-form content is more appropriate. Consistency is key. Maintain a consistent brand voice, visual style, and messaging across all your chosen channels to create a cohesive and recognizable identity.

Measuring your communication strategy's success entails more than just counting likes, shares, and how many people visit your website. As much as these tools are invaluable, the accurate measure of your success is changing lives and growing faith within your community. Are your people connecting to the church? Is spiritual growth taking place in their lives? And is your membership increasing with full involvement? These qualitative results serve as a better benchmark. Regularly take your congregation's pulse through surveys, focus groups, or casual conversations. Use that input to sharpen your communication strategy and effectively deliver what your community needs. Remember, church marketing is not a manipulation to get people to come to services; it's an authentic sharing of the good news of Jesus Christ and an invitation to others to experience the transforming power of faith.

Integrate prayer into your marketing. Seek God's guidance in choosing the proper channels, formulating your message, and gauging your progress. Pray for wisdom and discretion in your decisions, trusting God's leading. Consider organizing prayer meetings specifically for your church outreach work, inviting members to pray for the effectiveness of your communications and the people you wish to reach. This spiritual dimension ensures that your efforts are grounded in faith and aligned with God's will. Remember, your goal is to draw more people into the church to give glory to God and share his love. This overall goal should be the foundation for all your marketing efforts.

Therefore, when selecting appropriate communication channels for your church, you should carefully consider your target audience, available resources, and the message you want to convey. It's about strategically blending traditional and digital methods to create a cohesive and impactful approach. Authentic communication, consistent branding, and a prayerful approach will help you effectively reach those seeking a deeper connection with God while building a thriving, vibrant community of faith and love. Remember that continuous evaluation and adaptation are crucial to keeping your strategy up to date with the needs of your church and the changing digital landscape. Above all, may your marketing efforts mirror God's heart and relentless love toward everyone.

Creating Authentic and Engaging Content

Your created content is the heartbeat of active church marketing. This goes beyond just broadcasting; one should connect with others and cause a spiritual awakening in them through it. It involves genuinely understanding your audience, remaining transparent, and allowing room for creativity within the views of your church. The content you create should reflect the love and grace of God in a way that resonates with people on a personal level and compels them to take the following steps in their relationship with Jesus. First, consider your target audience. What are their interests, needs, and aspirations? What kind of language resonates with them? Are they primarily young families, seasoned adults, or a diverse mix of ages and backgrounds? Knowing your audience lets you craft your message for maximum effect. For example, a young adult base might be most receptive to short, engaging video content on social media. Conversely, older generations might find interest in a well-penned newsletter or even a podcast with deep discussions about faith and life. So, do not overlook demographic research.

Use general church data or light surveying to obtain the best insight into their wants and needs. Again, knowing how they receive information will significantly enhance an effective marketing campaign.

When you understand your audience, get more serious about creating narratives. People believe stories-especially stories that deal with their pain, successes, or hopes. Share your congregation members' testimonials of the transformative power of God. Feature the stories of individuals whose lives have been changed through your church's ministry. Highlight some of the positive impacts of your church in the community, such as service projects or outreach initiatives. Real-life stories resonate more than general announcements and build community through shared experience. Consider other storytelling formats: video interviews, written narratives, or dramatic presentations can be used to gain attention and communicate your message. Visuals are also one of the most essential pieces of engaging content. High-quality photographs and videos can make all the difference in how your message is received, primarily online. Invest in a professional photographer or videographer to capture events, ministries, and the faces of your congregation. Showcase the vibrant life of your church: the joy of worship, fellowship among members, and the tangible expression of God's love in action. Images that tell a story and evoke emotion are far more effective than generic stock photos or poorly lit videos. Remember to always get permission before using images or videos of people.

Consistency is key to keeping people engaged. Regularly posting updates, sharing inspiring messages, and providing relevant information keep your audience connected to your church and its activities. Develop a content calendar to schedule your posts and ensure a consistent flow of content across all your chosen platforms. It needs to be a fluid calendar that allows for spontaneous opportunities to share the Gospel, such as reacting to events in the local community or responding to topical discussions within social media. The key is to have a regular and relevant dialogue with your audience. Variety in format can help keep your audience's attention and prevent monotony. For instance, you can utilize blog posts, social media updates, videos, infographics, and podcasts.

Your content should genuinely reflect your church's values, beliefs, and mission. Avoid clichés or jargon that might feel insincere or out of touch with your audience. Instead, use clear, concise language expressing your message honestly and transparently. Authenticity builds trust, the foundation of any strong relationship between a church and its community. This means being transparent about your church's strengths and weaknesses, successes and challenges, and being willing to have tough conversations. Transparency creates a culture of openness and an authentic connection with your audience.

Interaction is key to having a thriving online community. Encourage comments, questions, and feedback from your audience. Respond to comments promptly and enter into meaningful conversations. Ask questions to stimulate dialogue and create a sense of community. Use interactive features like polls, Q&A sessions, and live streams to foster participation and increase engagement. Social media platforms are designed for interaction, and ignoring this aspect significantly limits their potential to build community and foster relationships. Actively participating in the online conversation demonstrates your willingness to listen, understand, and engage with your audience personally.

Always pray for guidance as you create and distribute your content. Seek God's wisdom in choosing the words, selecting images, and crafting the message for your content. Ask God to bless your efforts so that your content will reach those most in need of Him. Regular prayer should not be considered a mere formality but a vital part of the process, grounding your marketing efforts in faith and ensuring your content reflects your church's spiritual values. Seek feedback from trusted members of your church leadership team to ensure your content aligns with the church's overall mission and vision.

Creating authentic and engaging content for your church will involve understanding your audience, telling compelling stories, using strong visuals, being consistent, staying authentic, interacting, and always seeking God's guidance. Use church marketing to share the Gospel's transformative power by building a thriving, vibrant community centered in faith and love through thoughtfully crafting your message and engaging your community. This process requires dedication, prayer, and a willingness to adapt and refine your strategies as you learn what resonates most with your unique audience. Remember that the goal is to increase the numbers, nurture hearts, and grow souls closer to God. Your church marketing initiatives should not be defined alone by the numbers; the measurement of success has to move into individual life change and community growth in faith and love. A comprehensive approach helps create such means that genuinely reflect God's love and his purpose for the church. Ultimately, it is hoped that your marketing efforts will reflect a deep commitment to proclaiming the Gospel in a relevant and resonant way to those you seek to reach. The effectiveness of your strategies will be evidenced not just by increased attendance but by a genuine transformation of hearts and minds. This requires ongoing prayer, reflection, and commitment to serving God through your church's outreach efforts.

Chapter 3

Leveraging Digital Platforms for Outreach

Building a Strong Online Presence

In modern times, a strong web presence is no longer a luxury but a necessity for churches. It's the modern-day equivalent of a welcoming church building where people can explore your community, discover your message, and connect with your congregation. This requires a strategic and prayerful approach to building the presence, just as every aspect of your ministry is done with the same commitment to God's will. It's not about keeping up with the latest fads or emulating strategies that work for secular organizations; it's about using technology to spread the Gospel and genuinely connect people through faith.

Your website is the foundation of your web presence. Your website should feel like a virtual welcome mat- a place where community and connection are built. It needs to be easy to use, attractive, and simple to navigate, even for those who aren't tech-savvy. Avoid clutter and too much information. Make sure it is clear and concise. Your website should have your mission, values, and upcoming events. Include high-quality photos and videos showcasing the warmth and vibrancy of your community. Make sure the contact information is easy to find so visitors can quickly get in touch with you. You might want to add a blog for regular updates, thought-provoking articles, and inspirational stories from your congregation. This will help build community and give you great content to push out on your social media sites. Most importantly, make sure your site is mobile-friendly, as this is how most people access the internet nowadays via their smartphones and tablets. Investment in professional website design is well worth it for your importance in connecting with your community in the digital space. Regular updates and maintenance are vital to maintaining a clean, functional, and attractive online platform.

Social media presents a powerful opportunity for engagement and outreach. It's a dynamic landscape, with each platform offering unique strengths. Facebook, for instance, can be used to build a sense of community, sharing updates, photos, and event announcements. With its visual focus, Instagram enables you to share striking images and videos that tell your church's story in a visually captivating way. YouTube can share sermons, testimonies, and behind-the-scenes peeks into your church life. With its concise format, Twitter is the perfect avenue for sharing quick updates and inspirational quotes and participating in conversations relevant to faith and community. At the same time, it is essential to remember that social media should not be used merely as a broadcast medium. One must genuinely engage with followers. Timely responses to comments and messages, demonstrating an ability to listen and converse, are paramount. Conduct polls and Q&A sessions that provide an avenue for interaction and help build community. Create a content calendar to ensure you are posting consistently, keeping your presence regular, and showing the vibrancy of your community. Remember that the tone and content you share should be prayerfully considered, ensuring it aligns with your church's values and reflects God's love and compassion.

Email marketing is often overlooked but remains one of the most effective tools for consistent communication. It enables you to nurture relationships with existing members and reach prospective members who may have expressed interest in your church. It would be best to grow the list responsibly by respecting people's privacy and conforming to data protection regulations. Use your email list to keep in touch via regular newsletters, event announcements, and general information. Segment your list into groups of young adults, families with children, and senior citizens, and tailor your messages toward them. Personalize all your mailings where possible, affording a personal touch so that each subscriber will feel kept in mind and essential. Do not burden the subscribers with too many emails; sometimes less is more. Make an email's clear call to action to spur some activity or engagement. Monitor your email metrics for effectiveness and further opportunities. Ensure your emails are mobile-friendly and visually appealing, making them accessible and engaging for all recipients. Most importantly, let your email communications reflect the genuine care and compassion that defines your ministry.

Promote events on your website, social media platforms, and through email marketing. Design promotional materials with eye-catching appeal flyers, posters, and videos. Spread the word through all channels. Use event management tools to streamline the processes of registration and ticket purchase, making it easy for attendees. Live-stream events wherever possible to increase accessibility for a wider audience. Afterward, post photos and videos online for others to experience vicariously. Gather feedback from participants regarding the event's effectiveness to understand what went well and what didn't. Ensure that all participants can access your event, whether because of physical limitations or lack of technological capability. Consider having some events online and others in person to reach different audiences.

Website traffic, social media engagement, and email open rates are necessary, but these metrics don't fully capture the spiritual fruit of your labor. Instead of solely focusing on quantitative data, prioritize qualitative measures that reflect the growth and transformation within your community. Consider conducting surveys to gauge member satisfaction and identify areas for improvement. Seek feedback through informal conversations to understand the impact of your digital efforts on individuals' faith journeys. Monitor membership growth, church event participation, and small group engagement. Focus on the change of lives, not merely gathering statistics. True success is measured by building faith, discipleship growth, and expanding God's kingdom.

Building a strong online presence is a never-ending process that takes effort and prayerful reflection. Keep reviewing your strategies, adapting to changing trends, and ask your congregation for feedback. Leverage new technologies but never at the expense of authenticity and genuine connection. Remember, your goal is to expand your online presence, share the Gospel's transformative power, and build a thriving online community rooted in faith. By approaching digital outreach with prayer, intentionality, and a deep commitment to serving God, you can create a powerful online presence that glorifies Him and strengthens His kingdom. Like all aspects of ministry, this journey calls for patience, persistence, and trust in God's guidance. Through prayerful reflection and diligent application of these principles, your church can tap into the power of digital platforms as effective ways to reach and engage a greater community, extending God's love and grace into the digital world.

Utilizing Social Media for Connection

Effective social media use requires an intentional strategy beyond updating your status. It's about building relationships, sharing encouragement, and creating community. This isn't about jumping on every viral trend or trying to be like secular brands; rather, it is about utilizing these tools to organically share the Gospel and connect people where they are. Prayerful consideration should guide every aspect of your social media strategy, ensuring that your online presence reflects the values and mission of your church.

First, identify your target audience. Who are you trying to reach? Understand their demographics, interests, and online behavior to tailor your content and choose the appropriate platforms. Are you targeting young adults who are most active on Instagram and TikTok? Or is an older demographic more in your sights, perhaps with greater engagement on Facebook? Knowing your audience allows you to create targeted messages that resonate and invite engagement. This is not just a question of demographics; it's about understanding their spiritual journeys and needs. What are their questions? What are their struggles? What kind of hope are they seeking? Answering these questions will help you tailor your content to speak directly to their hearts.

Once you have identified your target audience, select the right platforms. Facebook remains a popular choice for many churches, providing a space for sharing announcements, events, and inspirational messages. With its focus on visual storytelling, Instagram can be effective for sharing photos and videos of church events, highlighting community outreach efforts, and showcasing the personal stories of your congregation members. YouTube is ideal for sharing sermons, teaching videos, and testimonies, potentially reaching a broader audience beyond your immediate community. Twitter can be used for quick updates, sharing inspirational quotes, and engaging in relevant conversations. But remember, it's not just enough to be on these channels; there has to be regular, engaging content to keep a strong online presence and find new followers. The contents should be varied and engaging. Don't limit yourself to mere announcements and events. Think about posting inspiring stories, quotes from scripture, reflections on faith with insight, and behind-the-scenes glimpses of life at the church. Use high-quality visuals and videos, and make sure your posts are well-written and understood. Keep your audience in mind when creating content. What will resonate with them? What questions are they asking? What kind of inspiration do they need? Incorporate different types of content, from short videos to longer blog posts, to keep your audience engaged and coming back for more.

Regular posting keeps your audience involved and reminds them of you. Create a content calendar to help you plan and schedule your posts in advance; this enables you to ensure a steady flow of fresh content and keeps gaps in online engagement minimal. Consider the best times for posting based on your audience's online activity. Take advantage of social media scheduling tools to help you do so consistently, even on days when you are committed to other things.

Interaction is key. Respond to comments and messages in a timely and thoughtful manner. Engage in conversations, answer questions, and build community with your followers. Demonstrate that you are genuinely interested in connecting with your audience. Respond to comments, even negative ones, with grace and respect. This shows your audience that you value their feedback and are committed to building a positive online community. Don't be afraid to ask questions that will stimulate interaction. Use polls, Q&A sessions, and live videos to connect with your audience personally.

Measure your success, but don't get bogged down in vanity metrics. While tracking metrics like follower count, likes, and shares is helpful, the ultimate measure of success is your social media efforts' impact on people's lives. Are people connecting with your church? Are they finding spiritual nourishment and encouragement through your online content? Are they getting involved in your ministry? Focus on building relationships and sharing the Gospel; the numbers will follow.

You can go ahead and pay to promote your posts on these networks. Both Facebook and Instagram have relatively affordable advertising options that allow you to target specific demographics or interests. This may be a mighty tool for broadening your reach to people who might never otherwise find your church online. Remember, it complements but does not replace your organic social media strategy. Let it not be that, while looking for numerical growth, this aspect overshadows the interaction based on authenticity and authentic engagement. Your online presence has to be genuinely faith-based and people-to-people.

Collaboration is key. Partner with other churches, ministries, and organizations to expand your reach and create meaningful cross-promotional opportunities. This increases your online visibility and fosters a sense of unity and collaboration within the broader Christian community. Find opportunities to collaborate with organizations that share your values and mission. This might involve co-hosting online events, sharing each other's content, or participating in joint initiatives.

Always remember that social media is a means, not the end. It is the means to reach out to people and share the Gospel, but again, it is not the real-life relationship and the involvement with the community. Use it wisely, pray over it, and let it reflect God's love and grace. It is not about accumulating followers or likes but about leading men to Christ and nurturing them into the faith.

Stay abreast of the latest trends and best practices. The digital landscape is ever-changing, so it's important to stay informed and adapt strategies along the way. Periodically evaluate your social media presence and ask for feedback from your congregation to make changes. Try new features and platforms, but always remember your core values and mission.

Don't be afraid to seek help from professionals. Many digital marketing agencies have a special place in their hearts for faith-based organizations. They can offer great strategy, content creation, and campaign management. Investing in professional services can be a worthwhile investment that will help you make the most of your online outreach efforts. Remember, seeking advice and support doesn't demonstrate weakness but rather a commitment to effective stewardship of your church's resources.

With prayer, intentionality, and a deep commitment to serving God, your church can have a robust online presence for His glory and the strengthening of His kingdom. In all its aspects, ministry requires patience, persistence, and trust in God's leading. Through prayerful reflection and diligent application of these principles, your church can tap into the power of digital platforms to effectively reach and engage a wider community, extending God's love and grace into the digital world. Always be authentic, genuinely connect, and be committed to serving others. Let your online presence reflect the Gospel's transformative power and the welcoming spirit of your

church community. This approach will foster a genuinely
flourishing online ministry.

Email Marketing Strategies for Engagement

When done with a strategic and prayerful approach,
email marketing becomes one of the most helpful ways to
nurture your church community and reach out to prospective
members. Unlike those quick social media posts that disappear
into the ether, emails are a more personal and direct way to
connect with your member base, fostering deeper connections
and regular, faith-bolstering messages. Newsletters alone aren't
enough. All this means you have to build a strong strategy based
on authenticity, value, and a deep understanding of the needs of
your congregation if you want to truly engage your audience and
ensure that this has a lasting impact. First, you have to build a
strong email list. It's not just about collecting email addresses.
You need to create a system that values data privacy and
transparency. Make your sign-up process easy and accessible,
and highlight what they'll get from signing up to your email list.
What will they receive? Will they be informed about events,
inspirational messages, or exclusive resource access? Be very
upfront and honest about this. Do not use devious or misleading
methods to capture subscribers. Consider offering an incentive,
such as a free e-book of sermons, access to exclusive online
resources, or a discount on an upcoming church event. But
remember, the incentive should always align with your church's
mission and values.

After collecting email addresses, you need to segment
your audience. Don't send out generic, mass emails. Instead,

group your subscribers based on demographics, interests, or levels of engagement. Are you targeting young adults, families, or senior citizens? Do they show interest in specific ministries or events? Tailoring your messages to particular segments ensures your content resonates with each group, maximizing engagement and minimizing the likelihood of unsubscribes. For example, a young adult group might appreciate emails with relevant social events and engaging discussions on faith and current issues. Meanwhile, senior citizens may want emails with information about senior programs, Bible studies that cater to their interests, and comforting spiritual messages.

This makes the content of your emails so important. Don't send overly promotional or sales-y emails. Provide value by sharing inspiring stories and devotional content, announcing events (with clear calls to action), and providing links to helpful resources. Attach high-quality images and videos to make your email visually appealing. Remember, this is not just to keep them informed but also to connect with them on a spiritual level.

Pay attention to the timing of your emails. Understand the behavior of your audience. At what time do they open and engage with their emails? Do some testing of days and times of the week to see what works best for your church. Do not bombard subscribers with emails. Most people can handle a weekly or bi-weekly newsletter. Of course, urgent announcements or timed things are fair game for other emails.

Constantly personalize your emails. Using the subscriber's name in a greeting personalizes it, and the content should reflect their interest in that particular segment. This will help you show them that they are important as individuals and can really connect them to you better.

Include a clear call to action in every email. What do you want your subscribers to do? Go to your website, sign up for an event, or donate. Make it easy for them by providing precise and concise instructions. Use strong action verbs and visually prominent buttons to encourage clicks.

Monitor your response. The email marketing application tracks key indicators such as open rates, click-through rates, and unsubscribes. This data will provide valuable insights regarding what is working and what needs improvement. Analyze your email campaigns from time to time to refine your strategy toward effectiveness. Don't just look at the number; the quality matters much more. A small-sized, highly engaged audience serves far better than an extensive and uninterested list.

Beyond just sending out newsletters, consider using email marketing for specific campaigns. You could send promotional emails for events such as a church picnic, concert, or special service. You could also do an email campaign that walks new members through your church structure and services to make them feel welcome and integrated into your faith community. Such focused campaigns are far more effective than general announcements.

Building lasting relationships with your community requires more than a one-way communication approach. Encourage two-way communication. Include an easy, straightforward way for people to respond to your emails: a reply button or link to a feedback form on your website. Use surveys and polls to understand your audience's needs and preferences better. Respond promptly and personally to emails you receive. This responsiveness shows that your ministry cares about its community personally.

A critical point of successful email marketing is compliance with data privacy regulations, such as GDPR or CCPA, whichever applies to your location. Get explicit consent for email subscriptions, give them an easy way to unsubscribe, and keep your email list secure. Be respectful of your subscribers' data and transparent with it. This is integrity on display, and trust is a core component of any community of people, including a church community.

Email complements your ministry, not replaces it. It adds to your interactions, conferences, and true community development inside the church walls. Email marketing is a prayer and deep commitment to serving God and His people. View each email as an opportunity to share the Gospel message, strengthen faith, and nurture relationships within your community.

Effective email marketing involves so much more than simply writing and sending messages. It is about building a meaningful relationship, adding value, and serving your congregation personally. By focusing on authenticity, personalization, and frequent engagement, you can use email marketing to build up your community and spread the transforming love of Christ to more people. Always pray for God's guidance with all your efforts and define success by the numbers and how His kingdom grows and flourishes. Let your emails reflect the grace and love of Jesus.

Online Event Promotion and Management

Building on the principles of authentic communication established in our email marketing discussion, let's dive into the dynamic world of online event promotion and management. In today's interconnected world, leveraging digital platforms to promote church events is not an option but necessary to reach a wider audience and maximize impact. However, it is just not enough to put an event on Facebook. Successful online event promotion is all about strategy rooted in prayer and clearly understanding your target audience. First, define the objectives of your event. What are you trying to accomplish? Are you trying to build community, raise awareness for a cause, or introduce new members to your church? Well-defined goals inspire your promotional strategy and allow you to measure success in attendance and, more profoundly, in the lives of people and the community. This is a time for prayerful discernment. Seek God's guidance regarding your event's purpose, timing, and direction.

Once you have defined your objectives, it will be essential to determine who your target audience is. Who are you trying to reach? Understanding their demographics, interests, and online habits will help you tailor your messaging and choose the most effective platforms. Are you trying to get young adults, families, or a particular demographic within the community? This will guide you on what social media platforms to use, how to set the tone for your messaging, and what the aesthetic of your promotional materials will look and feel like. For instance, a youth event might thrive on Instagram and TikTok, while a more traditional event might benefit from Facebook and email marketing.

Creating compelling event pages on relevant platforms is paramount. Don't just list the date, time, and location. Craft a description that captures the essence of the event and speaks directly to the target audience. Showcase the event's atmosphere with high-quality images and videos, highlighting what makes it unique. What is it about your unique event? What's unique is the powerful message, uplifting music, time of fellowship, or serving others. Highlight those aspects to draw people in. Include clear calls to action, such as "Register now," "RSVP," or "Learn more," in which people can take their next step.

Social media provides a powerful tool arsenal for event promotion. Each platform has nuances, and the multidimensional approach is often the most effective. With its extensive user base and robust event creation features, Facebook remains a cornerstone of online event promotion. Create a Facebook Event page for your event, invite people, post updates, and encourage engagement. Visual-centric Instagram is ideal for showcasing the beauty and energy of your church and events. Use high-quality images and videos, employing relevant hashtags to expand your reach. Consider running targeted ads to reach a specific audience segment.

With its real-time nature, Twitter is excellent for spreading quick announcements and engaging in conversations about the event. Use relevant hashtags and interact with other users to create a buzz that expands reach. LinkedIn can be a great way to reach professionals and community leaders. Highlight how the event relates to their professional and personal interests. A powerful video platform, YouTube allows posting event highlights, testimonials, and behind-the-scenes moments that help build anticipation and excitement for an event. TikTok's very short-form video format provides exceptional value in reaching younger audiences. Use creative, engaging videos that capture attention and bring life and excitement to your event. Beyond organic social media, let's consider the power of paid advertising. With Facebook, Instagram, and Google Ads, you have options to run targeted ads: demographic targeting based on location, interests, and many other factors. Paid advertising requires some budget, but it greatly expands your reach and can drive registrations to your events. Carve out a thoughtful budget for ads and monitor them to see where to leverage your funds best. Always make sure any advertising reflects your church's values and mission.

Equally important is managing registrations and communication. Employing online registration tools streamlines this process, allowing for data capture of key information while offering a user-friendly interface that easily integrates into your social media platforms. Regular email updates to attendees registered or otherwise, can maintain interest in event details, schedules, and last-minute changes. This continues the anticipation and creates a community with the attendees.

Interactive elements can help elevate your online event promotion. Consider online Q&A sessions, running contests or giveaways, or creating polls to generate excitement. Live streaming of the event, or parts of it, lets people unable to attend in person be a part of it, thereby increasing your reach and a sense of inclusiveness. These interactive elements are essential to create interest and sustain excitement.

Post-event communication is a must after the event. Thank the guests with thank-you emails for attending the event. Photos and videos of the event can be shared on social media, creating a sense of community and shared experience. Request feedback from attendees to gain insights for future events. Such continuous engagement will ensure that the momentum created by the event does not get lost but is continued for a long time, increasing participation in future events and broader church outreach.

Measuring the success of your online event promotion shouldn't solely focus on the number of attendees. While attendance is necessary, consider the qualitative aspects as well.

Did the event achieve its intended objectives? Did it foster community, raise awareness, or introduce new members to your church? Gather feedback from attendees, both online and offline, to assess the impact of the event and identify areas for improvement. Prayerful reflection is essential, as it allows you to discern the hand of God in whether or not the event went well and how you can do things differently in the future. The digital landscape is forever changing. Keeping up with the latest developments and trends is essential in keeping your online presence relevant. Try new tools and techniques and adjust your strategy according to your audience's response and feedback. Most importantly, keep a spirit of prayer and discernment in all your efforts. Let your online event promotion reflect God's love and grace, a faithful witness to His transformative power. Seek His guidance in every aspect of your planning and execution, trusting in His provision and wisdom. Success is ultimately not about metrics and numbers but about lives touched and transformed through the love of Christ. Let your digital strategies be an extension of your heart to share His message with the world.

Measuring Digital Impact Ethically

Measuring the effectiveness of our digital outreach is a unique challenge within the context of church ministry. While traditional marketing often focuses on quantifiable results, such as website traffic, social media engagement, and email open rates, as ministers, our focus must remain steadfast on spiritual impact. We are not selling a product; we are sharing the transformative message of the Gospel. Therefore, our metrics must reflect this profound difference.

The temptation to latch onto superficial numbers- the number of likes, shares, or comments on a post is intense. These metrics can create a false sense of accomplishment, leading us to believe that many interactions equate to genuine spiritual growth. Yet, a viral social media post doesn't necessarily equate to a transformed life. A thousand likes on a Facebook post regarding a sermon may indicate broad reach, but it doesn't tell us how many hearts were truly touched or how many lives were changed by the message.

Ethical measurement requires a shift in perspective. We need to move beyond vanity metrics and focus on indicators that reflect the true objectives of our outreach. Instead of just counting followers, we should be measuring meaningful engagement. This might include comment analysis to determine comprehension or whether a person has taken a step toward faith. For instance, did someone request prayer, attend a service after an online announcement, or start a discipleship path after interacting with online content?

Website analytics could be employed. While website traffic and page views can be measured, which is immensely valuable, the real value will be understanding why people are coming to the site. Are they seeking spiritual answers? Are they seeking community or support? Are they browsing? This qualitative data can be more revealing than knowing how many visitors there have been. This requires a more considered study of the content consumed and how users interact with the website's features and downloads to participate in online forums.

Email marketing offers a different kind of insight. While open and click-through rates are helpful, they only tell part of the story. The more important metric is whether the email's message led to meaningful interaction. Did recipients respond to a call to action? Did they register for a discipleship program or volunteer opportunity? Did they forward the email to a friend? These are far better indicators of successful communication than mere open rates. Further, focusing on delivering personalized, thoughtful messages to particular segments of your congregation has the added benefit of better relationships and deeper engagement, which is also a lot more ethical and spiritually rewarding than mass-mailing generic content.

Social media analytics are another kettle of fish altogether. Measuring engagement in likes and shares is superficial. A more ethical approach would be carefully assessing the quality of comments and conversations. Are people engaging in respectful and informative discussions? Are they sharing their faith journeys openly and honestly? Are there opportunities for real connection and community building? Instead, look for the signs of spiritual growth and connection among your online community for a more meaningful picture of the success of your strategy. And always remember that social media is a tool, not a goal. Its purpose is to further the Kingdom of God, not to amass followers.

Live-streaming services and online events offer another lens to assess digital impact. While it is easy to track viewing numbers, the question is if the service engages and impacts its viewers. Did the virtual church translate into new physical attendees? Did online audiences resonate with the message on different levels that positively affected changes in their views or lifestyles? Did they perhaps continue seeking more through online discussion forums or participating in other follow-up activities? These are qualitative elements of success, far more important than simple counts of views. Post-event surveys can be beneficial in gathering feedback and getting a sense of audience responses and feelings. These show if the message of an event came through and inspired deeper engagement.

Beyond analytics, ethical measurement must include qualitative metrics. Are people spiritually growing due to our digital outreach? Are they closer to God? Are they relating on a deeper level with other believers? Are they serving and showing compassion to others? These are the ultimate measures of success. Consider using personal testimonies, feedback forms, and one-on-one conversations to gather this crucial information. Conducting interviews with people engaged with your digital content provides more prosperous, more profound insights than simply observing quantitative metrics. By listening carefully and prayerfully, you can gain a valuable understanding of the lives you are impacting.

Measuring digital impact ethically requires a shift in mindset. We must abandon a purely results-oriented approach and embrace a holistic perspective, prioritizing spiritual growth and genuine connection. We are called to be stewards of God's grace, and our digital efforts must reflect this sacred responsibility. Prayerful reflection, ongoing assessment, and dedication to genuine connectivity are crucial in ensuring that our digital strategies serve and do not detract from our mission to share God's love and transform lives. It is not about the numbers but building the Kingdom of God, one soul at a time.

Evaluate your strategies regularly. What's working? What's not? How could you create more spiritual depth for the people from what they will do online with your ministry? Do you foster an online community in a meaningful way? Everything happening within the digital context changes so fast. Your regular evaluation should continue toward betterment with relevant quantitative and qualitative data on board. Ultimately, digital impact from an ethical point of view is a process of continuing to learn and be refined through prayer and deep devotion to serving the needs of others in Christ's name. Through this process, refinement and growth continue toward a more effective and faithful reflection of God's love and grace in the digital arena. It becomes an act of worship, a striving incontinently to align our work with God's purpose and plan.

Chapter 4

Engaging Your Local Community

Identifying Community Needs and Opportunities

Identifying the needs of your community is the backbone of effective outreach. This is not about the imposition of your church's agenda but understanding the context in which God has placed you and how you can best be His hands and feet in that place. It includes a multifaceted approach as one moves beyond observation to deeply understand their neighbors' hopes, fears, and realities. Know that your community is diverse and comprises people of different backgrounds, ages, socio-economic statuses, and cultural experiences. One-size-fits-all rarely works; what is required is subtlety and nuances.

One compelling approach is a deep and comprehensive community needs assessment. This is not an event per se but an ongoing process of data collection and interpretation through the eyes of faith. Consider using multiple strategies to gain an overall understanding. Observe first. Be out in your community. Go to the parks, attend community events (even when not church-sponsored events), and strike up casual conversations with people. Note what you repeatedly see as concerns, needs, and opportunities. Do you notice poverty, homelessness, or addiction? Are there under-resourced populations, such as the elderly and marginalized groups? What kinds of businesses thrive or struggle in the area? These observations can provide valuable insights into your community's health and needs.

Supplement observational studies with data collection. Utilize readily available resources such as census data, local government reports, and studies conducted by community organizations. This data can provide demographic information, identify areas of high need, and uncover specific challenges affecting your community. For example, census data may outline age distribution, income levels, and educational attainment, to which you could specifically target outreach. The local government may issue reports on crime rates, unemployment, and access to healthcare, giving much-needed context for outreach programs. Surveys and Interviews Besides officially released data, try to get information directly through surveys and interviews. Surveys can be conducted online, in person, or by mail, depending on your community's demographics and accessibility. Keep questions focused and straightforward and consider including quantitative (multiple-choice) and qualitative (open-ended) questions to gather various perspectives. Interviews provide an even deeper level of insight: one-on-one conversations with community members allow you to better understand their experiences, needs, and perspectives. Actively listen and ask follow-up questions; your goal is to collect data and establish genuine connections with your community.

Partner with local organizations and community leaders to enhance your understanding. Libraries, schools, social service agencies, and local businesses often possess valuable insights into community needs. Collaborate with them; their expertise and established networks can significantly enhance your assessment. Consider participating in local community meetings and forums. These gatherings often bring out information on community issues and needs, which may give insight into unmet

needs in your community that your church can serve.
Relationships you build with local leaders, such as school
principals, city council members, and nonprofit organization
heads, can create avenues of cooperation and sharing of
resources. They can offer key insight and advice.

Discernment and prayer are used to interpret the data
that has been collected. Animate the information you have
gathered from all sources by carefully analyzing and looking for
patterns and recurring themes. Identify areas where your
church's strengths and resources can best meet the needs within
the community. Pray for guidance to discern the needs most
closely align with your church's mission and vision. Remember,
you are not called to solve all the problems but to focus your
attention and energy on areas where you can make a difference
and be faithful to your calling.

Prioritize needs by urgency, impact, and feasibility. Not
every need you identify will be something your church can
realistically address. You will need to prioritize them based on
the urgency of urgent crisis relief versus long-term community
development, the potential impact of your intervention, and the
feasibility of your church's involvement-available resources,
volunteer capacity, and expertise. These careful prioritizations
will ensure that your resources are used most effectively and
your outreach initiatives can be sustained.

For instance, if there is a significant need in your
community for after-school programs for children, you might
initiate a program at your church or collaborate with an existing
one. Such a program would provide homework help, recreational
activities, and mentorship. If the needs assessment points to food
insecurity, your church can establish a food pantry, partner with
a local food bank, or hold weekly meals for the community. If you
find that many of your elderly are isolated, you might initiate a

visitation program whereby volunteers are coordinated to visit and be companions. This way, you can focus on key areas of need and not spread your resources too thin.

Document your findings and share them with your church leadership and congregation. Write a clear, concise report summarizing your community needs assessment. This document must include key findings, prioritized needs, and proposed outreach initiatives. Share this report with your church leadership to gain support and collaboration for the planned initiatives. Transparency is key; this document should be used to inform and inspire your congregation to participate actively in community engagement.

Identifying community needs is never done; go back to your assessment regularly and refine your strategies as needed. As your community continues to change, so too will its needs. Remain flexible, adaptable, and open to the guidance of the Holy Spirit as He directs your efforts and leads you to serve in ways that honor Him and bless your neighbors. Prayer will lead from initial observation to implementing outreach programs, seeking God's will and guidance. He is the source of all good things, and His wisdom will make a difference in effectiveness and impact in community engagement. You aim to reflect His love and compassion in tangible ways, showing how the Gospel has transformed your heart and is now transforming the life of your community. This deep connection with God will ensure that your efforts are not just acts of service but expressions of His grace.

Organizing Community Events and Outreach Programs

With an understanding of needs within the community, a logical next step involves creating community events and outreach that genuinely meet those needs and mirror His love. This isn't about making some flashy show but rather an event to help people see that this church is serious about ministering to others in realistic and meaningful ways. The compelling events are thoughtfully planned, strategically executed, and deeply rooted in prayer. They should drive the desire to build a relationship, share the Gospel subtly yet effectively, and create ways for them to get into an authentic relationship. Begin the planning process by listing specific needs within the community and then aligning some potential events to reach those needs directly. For example, if you have defined food insecurity as a concern, organizing a community food drive or a monthly soup kitchen could be highly impactful. Similarly, providing resources or workshops on budgeting and financial literacy could prove invaluable if many families struggle financially. Suppose you've discovered a lack of safe recreational activities for children and youth. In that case, some impactful outreach opportunities might be organizing sports days, arts and crafts sessions, or mentoring programs.

Beyond providing immediate needs, think of events that build community and social cohesion: family fun days, community picnics, neighborhood clean-up initiatives, or interfaith dialogue gatherings. The goal is to create welcoming spaces where individuals from diverse backgrounds can connect, interact, and feel a sense of belonging. This fosters a sense of trust and opens doors for more meaningful interactions and opportunities to share the Gospel.

The chosen event type will need to consider demographics and community preferences. What works in one community may not be as effective in another. For instance, a community with many young families would probably respond well to a children's carnival. On the other hand, communities with large elderly populations would respond more to a senior citizens' luncheon or health fair focused on their needs. Research and sensitivity make your events genuinely inclusive and well-received.

Logistics also play an important role in event organization: finding an appropriate venue, obtaining permits if needed, organizing volunteers, managing resources, and establishing a communications system. In this respect, volunteer coordination is crucial to the event's success. Make the atmosphere friendly and comfortable for your volunteers, train them properly, clearly indicate their responsibilities, and show appreciation for their help. Communication and keeping volunteers informed about schedules, tasks, and plan changes are also essential.

Another essential aspect is promotion. Promotion is more than just posters and announcements over the church PA system. It requires a broader platform to get the word out to those who need to know. Social media, local newspapers, community boards, flyers placed in the right strategic locations, and collaborations with other regional entities can be significant vehicles for this. Word-of-mouth referrals are also effective, as they indicate strong relationships among community members.

Crucially, every event should have a clear spiritual objective. While the primary focus may be on serving the community, opportunities for subtle yet authentic Gospel sharing should be woven into the fabric of the event. This could involve a short prayer or blessing, sharing a relevant Bible verse, or simply demonstrating the love and compassion of Christ through your actions and interactions. Remember, your actions often speak louder than words; be conscious of your behavior and the message you are portraying to the community you serve.

Follow-up after the event is essential, and it includes continuous improvement. Collect feedback from participants, volunteers, and organizers of the event. Analyze what worked, what did not work, and any lessons you can learn from this for future events. This will go a long way in shaping and refining future outreach programs and events. You may collect feedback using surveys, focus groups, or conversations to ensure ongoing relevance and impact.

Outreach programs are not limited to one-time events. Consider creating ongoing programs that regularly serve the community. These may be weekly Bible studies, regular mentorship programs for at-risk youth, support groups for those struggling with addiction, or community garden projects. These ongoing programs show consistency in commitment to the community and build deeper relationships.

When planning ongoing programs, remember to focus on sustainability. Establish clear goals, secure necessary resources, and build a strong team of volunteers and leaders who share your vision. Develop a system for tracking progress, evaluating outcomes, and adapting the program as needed. A well-structured program will impact the community, fostering hope, growth, and spiritual transformation.

Partnership with other organizations and churches is key. Collaboration expands your reach, resources, and impact. This kind of partnership can leverage the network of local charities, schools, businesses, and churches, creating some synergy. In such cases, joint events or sharing of resources cut down drastically on the workload for individual organizations while raising overall community impact. Allow respectful and collaborative relationships with partners, allowing them to maintain their mission and goals.

Community events and outreach aim to bring people into a church to share the transformed love of Christ. Concretely, it includes expressing God's grace through compassionate means of building friendships and providing avenues for spiritual development. Each encounter or event, along with programming, must be bathed in prayer, having complete dedication to reflect God's character in everything you put your hands to. Always seek God in every part of your direction, trust His wisdom, and step out in service to your community.

Measuring the success of community engagement efforts requires a shift in perspective. It is not solely about the number of attendees or the money raised. Instead, focus on the lives touched, the relationships built, and the positive impact on the community. Qualitative assessments, such as participant testimonials, anecdotal evidence of changed lives, and observations of strengthened community bonds, are invaluable in evaluating the actual effectiveness of your outreach initiatives. These qualitative measures give a more complete and accurate assessment than the quantitative data.

You will learn to effectively reach your community by consistently assessing and refining your strategies. Remember, community engagement is a marathon, not a sprint. It takes persistence, adaptability, and a deep commitment to serving others to achieve success over the long term. Your commitment will demonstrate God's love and compassion, paving the way for spiritual growth and transformation within your community. Let us never forget that the kingdom of God is built not on great campaigns but on millions of acts of love and service, reflecting His grace and mercy. Through these daily interactions, we make disciples and friends while furthering the growth of God's kingdom.

Building Relationships with Community Leaders

Building relationships with community leaders is crucial to effective church outreach. It's about more than just finding a place to hold an event; it's about developing partnerships where respect, mutual purpose, and collaboration in service are birthed in the love of Christ. This takes excellent intentionality, patience, and a willingness to serve with-not just utilize-community leaders. Read the following steps to discover how to identify key community leaders. This is a wide range: school principals and teachers, local business owners, representatives from non-profit organizations, city council members, police officers, fire department personnel, and even leaders of other faith communities. Don't limit your scope; consider who holds influence and respect within your area. A comprehensive approach ensures a broader reach and avoids overlooking potential allies in your ministry. For instance, developing a relationship with a local school principal can open doors for volunteer opportunities within the school, leading to increased visibility and chances to share the church's positive influence on the lives of students and their families. Likewise, partnerships with local businesses may provide opportunities to sponsor events, offer resources, and even create meaningful employment avenues for church members.

Once you've identified potential partners, begin the process of relationship building. This is not a transactional endeavor; it requires genuine investment. Start by simply introducing yourselves. Attend community events, volunteer your time at local initiatives, and actively listen to the needs and concerns expressed by community leaders. Show genuine interest in their work, their challenges, and their aspirations. This initial stage of relationship building is crucial. Do not immediately sell church events or programs; invest time building relationships and trust. For example, if the local food bank has few volunteers, you can offer your church's services for no other reason than to serve. This says much about your motives and positions you as a trustworthy partner.

After the initial contact, continue to communicate regularly. This may be through regular email, phone calls, or casual meetings. Also, inform them about your church's upcoming functions, campaigns, and activities. Be more focused on stories that show the difference caused by their help, combined with your prayerfulness. The repeated touching base will develop confidence and seriousness in your promise of communication. Consider personalized notes or cards based on their achievements and awards to the community. Small actions like this grease the wheels for effective relations. Remember, consistency is key to establishing meaningful long-term partnerships.

Collaborate on shared initiatives. Once trust has been established, actively seek opportunities for collaboration. This could involve co-hosting events, sponsoring community projects, or partnering on fundraising initiatives. When planning collaborative efforts, ensure that the vision aligns with the church's mission and the community's needs. For example, a collaboration between the church and a secular youth center might be a community sports day, providing activities and an organic opportunity for people to get to know each other. The goal is to find initiatives that are of mutual benefit to the community at large, not simply to promote the church.

Listen regularly. Good communication is the bedrock of any successful relationship. Regularly solicit input from community leaders, asking for their insights on how the church can better serve the community. Their perspectives will refine your outreach strategies and demonstrate your willingness to learn and adapt. This act of humility will strengthen your bonds and showcase your commitment to being a responsive and integral part of the local landscape. Consider periodic surveys or less formal feedback sessions to elicit their thoughts and experiences actively. Building a relationship requires time; this isn't a quick fix but a deep, long-term commitment that necessitates patience, persistence, and a heart of service. Be wary of expecting immediate success or the desire for speed-of-light wins. Instead, nurture the relationships in steady support and through life change found in Christ alone, demonstrated in your actions. Remember the parable of the Sower: some seeds take longer to sprout than others. Similarly, some relationships may develop more slowly than others.

Celebrate successes together. When joint initiatives reap positive results, they celebrate with one another. This knits the partners together through a shared success. Sometimes, formally or informally, celebrating the two organizations will nurture friendship and build value within your partnership. Recognition and appreciation can boost motivation and stimulate further collaboration.

Building relationships with community leaders is not about manipulating them to support the church but instead partnering with them in serving the common good. Be a light in the darkness and hope for that which is hopeless, showing that your church is concerned for the welfare of your community, and you will find the landscape of your local area changed. This is where the actual effectiveness of your outreach lies in self-promotion but in selfless service. This perfectly aligns with God's call to love our neighbors, reflecting His character and the transformative power of His love in concrete ways.

Let your interactions be driven by a genuine will to serve, learn, and grow with the community leaders. Consider these relationships not merely as a means to an end but as opportunities to live out Christ's teachings and to create a dynamic, flourishing community based on faith and service. Each interaction is an opportunity to show the church's commitment to the holistic well-being of the community, building trust and mutual respect. Approach relationships with humility, transparency, and a commitment to service, and you will promote the church while leaving lasting positive impacts that extend far beyond the church's walls. This will provide a foundation for genuine growth, enabling the Gospel to be firmly rooted in and among your community. The strategy here is to engage in profound partnership-including respect for one another, mutual values, and a commitment to serving together in community life. Churches could do a much better job at extending their reach and increasing their positive influence, becoming the likeness of Christ's love and grace within their local communities by building relationships, genuinely listening to each other, maintaining consistent communication, and establishing joint ventures. It is not about how many are coming into the church. Still, genuine connections were forged, lives were touched positively, and the community was built out of selfless acts and steadfast faith that correctly measured an entity's success. This represents the essence of God's outreach: not a plan of metrics but one driven by love, compassion, and the pure desire to serve others in Christ's name.

Partnering with Local Businesses and Organizations

Expanding this authentic relationship development from community leaders to other local businesses and organizations creates a unique opportunity for this church to extend its influence by concretely demonstrating Christ's love. It's not about leveraging whatever means one can; the best model is mutually advantageous and reflects the nature of the Kingdom of God's partnerships. The success depends on engaging in conversations with organizations whose core values connect to the church's mission and offering reciprocal support.

First, identify some potential partners. Think of local businesses that share values similar to your church's, such as community development, social responsibility, or family values. Don't think only the obvious; a local bakery may be willing to donate baked goods for a church function, while a bookstore may host a book signing with a Christian author. Likewise, partnerships with non-profit organizations should be investigated. Food banks, homeless shelters, and community centers often share the church's passion for serving the vulnerable. In partnering with such groups, the church accesses resources, increases its credibility in the community, and proves - quite literally - that it is committed to serving people in practical, tangible ways.

Building these partnerships requires an intentional process. It won't happen if the church waits for businesses or organizations to knock on its door. A simple phone call, email, or in-person meeting can lay the foundation for a fruitful partnership. During these initial interactions, emphasize the mutual benefits of collaboration. For instance, a partnership with a local restaurant might involve the church hosting a fundraising event, benefiting the church's fundraising efforts and patronage. Equally, the partnership with a local radio station could also help the church announce upcoming events or broadcast sermons, increasing its visibility to more people.

Healthy partnerships depend on effective communication. Regular communication, whether via email, phone calls, or face-to-face meetings, keeps both parties on the same page regarding goals, expectations, and responsibilities. Be transparent: openly share the church's mission and goals and be open to hearing the organization's needs and objectives. This open line of communication will build trust and create a solid foundation for a long-term partnership.

Beyond the practical levels of resource sharing and co-organizing events, personal touch should always be used to forge relationships. These partnerships must be grounded in shared values and a common desire to serve the community. Consider inviting representatives from partner organizations to church events and vice versa. Social interaction at this level will bring camaraderie and help cement the church with its partners.

These partnerships should not be quantified merely by how much money has been acquired or how many people have attended. Success should be quantified by its impact on the community, the number of lives it touches, and, more importantly, the greater glory to God. Did the event feed the hungry? Give hope to the desperate? Strengthen the ties in the community. These qualitative measures are far more significant than quantifiable metrics.

To illustrate the potential of these partnerships, let's consider a few practical examples. A church could partner with a local coffee shop to host a weekly Bible study, providing a welcoming and relaxed atmosphere for attendees. This benefits the church by creating a new outreach opportunity and the coffee shop by attracting new customers. Likewise, the local sporting goods store might offer the church a chance to sponsor a youth sports team in exchange for the possibility of ministry to young people and increased church visibility within the community. The local theatre might engage the church in staging a faith-based play that utilizes the artistic talents of the church and provides a worthwhile experience for the community. These examples give testimony to the variety of options that become more concretely possible when congregations intentionally pursue and work to develop partnerships with a range of local businesses or organizations.

Another tactical step is to use volunteers with professional expertise in marketing, design, and accounting, for example, by offering their services free of charge to the partner organization. Thus, this creates a win-win situation whereby the partner organization gets valuable aid while the church members can use their gifts for God's glory. Through this spirit of service and collaboration, the partnership is usually strengthened, and solid relationships are fostered within the church community.

The church can advertise the business partner's products or services on its website, newsletters, or social media channels. The company could reciprocate by publicizing church events or activities. This mutually beneficial arrangement can significantly heighten both entities' visibility within the community. This kind of collaborative marketing works when it feels organic and authentic and doesn't feel forced or exploitative.

It is essential, however, to remember that not all partnerships will be successful. Some may only marginally impact the organization, while others may be problematic because of value or priority differences. The church should be judicious in selecting partners and prepared to disengage from partnerships inconsistent with the church's mission or values. It is not about forcing the partnerships to extend their reach but building healthy, mutual relationships. Remember, the focus should remain on building relationships that reflect the love and grace of Christ and genuinely serve the community.

As churches enter these partnerships, they must be clear about who they are and their mission. They must not lose their values to suit the preferences of the partnering organizations. Instead, they should seek partners who share their commitment to serving God and the community. This requires careful discernment and a willingness to walk away from partnerships that do not align with the church's core values. The goal is to create mutually beneficial and spiritually fulfilling relationships. It is about building a community of believers and impacting the broader community through shared values and collective purpose. The mission should always be in focus: sharing the love of Christ and building the kingdom of God.

Partnering with local businesses and organizations offers a powerful strategy for expanding the church's reach and impact. Building genuine relationships, opening communications, and prioritizing mutual benefit can create a robust network of support that goes far beyond the church walls. The rewards are not numerical but spiritual, relational, and community-based, reflecting the very essence of God's outreach plan. Success is measured not merely in the numbers but in lives changed and a community empowered through faith and service. This is not marketing; it's missional living, mirroring the selfless love of Christ in the heart of the community.

Serving the Underserved in Your Community

And in our genuine relationship-building, which extends beyond local businesses and organizations, the most vulnerable in our communities are not an exception. Serving the under-resourced is not simply charitable; it directly reflects Christ's love and is a powerful evangelistic tool. It's a living manifestation of Matthew 25:31-46, where Jesus emphasizes care for the least of these as the direct reflection of service unto Him. This involves identifying the specific needs within your community and tailoring your outreach to meet those needs effectively.

A crucial first step is conducting a thorough community needs assessment. This isn't a superficial exercise; it requires genuine engagement with local organizations, social services, and individuals. Speak to homeless shelters, food banks, domestic violence support groups, and other organizations that serve marginalized populations. Attend community meetings, town hall forums, and local council meetings to understand the prevailing issues better. Go beyond the reports and statistics to engage directly with those experiencing hardship to understand their needs and challenges firsthand. This direct interaction will inform your church's outreach strategies more effectively than any research report.

When you have a better understanding of the needs in your community, you can begin to think about how to respond effectively. This may include but is not limited to starting a food bank or soup kitchen, providing clothes or personal care items, offering job training, or arranging transportation. It may include mental health services, referral to lawyers, or educational resources that would equip the less fortunate. Be proactive in tailoring your services to the needs identified. Consider the unique challenges facing the elderly, the disabled, single mothers, recent immigrants, and those struggling with addiction. Each group has specific needs, and a generalized approach will be less practical than a carefully targeted response.

However, simply providing material assistance isn't enough. The goal is to meet immediate needs and build genuine relationships that foster spiritual growth. As you serve, listen to the stories and struggles of the people you're serving. Show empathy, respect, and compassion, avoiding judgmental attitudes or paternalistic approaches. Approach each interaction with a sincere desire to understand their perspective and offer support without imposing your beliefs. The power of your service doesn't just come from the practical help you provide but also from the love and acceptance you show in the process.

Building relationships involves intentional and consistent effort, which consists of establishing regular opportunities for service and a volunteer team to serve. This includes proper training for the volunteers by equipping them with practical skills to do the service and emotional intelligence in showing respect and compassion to whom they will serve. Role-playing can be effective in equipping volunteers with how to handle difficult situations. Also, discuss potential difficulties, develop strategies for de-escalation and conflict resolution, and give your volunteers proactive training to empower them confidently.

Consider developing partnerships with other groups currently serving the underserved. It's about collaboration. You can be infinitely more effective by combining resources and competencies with others who have already gained broad experience, such as local charities, social service agencies, and community centers. It also reduces overlap of work and optimizes resources used. This way, through collaborations, you'll develop an intertwined web for various supports to be made.

It is very important to measure the effectiveness of your outreach program. Certainly, quantifiable metrics-such as the number of meals served or items distributed-offer valuable information. It is equally important to evaluate the qualitative impact of your efforts. Are you developing significant relationships? Are you facilitating spiritual growth? Do you see changes in your lives? Ongoing feedback is very important from volunteers and those receiving service. Carry out surveys, focus groups, and personal interviews to better understand the impact of the program. This qualitative data is as important, if not more important, than the quantitative data.

Think about the ramifications of your service projects and initiatives. Solutions must be sustainable. Do not develop dependencies; rather, your goal is to make a person independent. This includes job training, educational opportunity, mentoring, and financial planning. Your objective is to give the individual the access and ability to overcome those things that have held them in states of poverty and dependency. This may be more of a long-term focus, but illustrates a dedication to authentic transformation, as opposed to shorter-term alleviation to full empowerment.

Serving the underserved is one way to worship. In itself, it is the concretion of God's love in action. A cornerstone in your outreach ministry should be prayer. Plead for guidance on what needs to be done, wisdom on how to achieve it through programs, and strength for volunteers. Also, pray for those you reach out to-that God bless and grant grace in their lives. Let your service be a testimony to God's love and compassion toward all people, especially those marginalized and forgotten. Your actions will speak volumes louder than words, reflecting a real commitment to serving Christ through serving others. The success of your outreach isn't measured by the number of people served but by the transformative power of God's love working through you to change hearts and lives. This is a commitment to the poor that will continue to enrich the lives of the ones you serve, yet will also profoundly bless your church community, deepening your faith and strengthening the bond with one another and Christ. This missional living is not an accessory added to your church activities, but it is rather at the heart of your witness to the world. It is the very embodiment of the Gospel message, a living testament to the power of God's grace.

Chapter 5

Developing a Sustainable Outreach Plan

Setting Measurable Goals and Objectives

Putting a sustainable outreach plan together will take much more than pure intent. It will entail strategy at its best-actual, effectual prayers coupled with the clear undertaking of a church's mission. That all begins to happen with setting goals that are specific, attainable, relevant, and time-bound (SMART). You are not merely desiring things to increase; you really must have some concrete, doable steps toward them. Think of it like plotting the course for your ship so you are not simply sailing around but actually heading in a specific direction. First, there is the alignment of your goals with the mission and vision of your church. What is the big idea of your church? Is it to reach the unchurched in your community? To go deeper in discipleship among your members? To be a provider of essential social services? Your goals need to support this general purpose directly. Suppose the mission of your church is to be a beacon of hope in a neighborhood in struggle. In that case, the outreach goals may revolve around community service, like starting a food bank or a mentorship program for youth. These goals, however, must be quantifiable. Instead of aiming vaguely for "increased community engagement," define a specific, measurable objective like, "Increase participation in our community food bank by 25% within the next year."

Measurable objectives vary significantly depending on your church's size, resources, and context. A large, well-resourced church might set ambitious goals around building new facilities or launching extensive international mission programs. Such a church might establish a goal to "Raise $500,000 in donations for the construction of a new community center within two years." On the other hand, a smaller church with limited resources may want to focus on strengthening the internal community and increasing member involvement. A reachable goal for such a church could be to "Increase weekly attendance by 10% within six months by implementing a new small group ministry program."

After you have established broad, overarching goals aligned with your mission, break those into smaller and more manageable objectives. These must be specific and easily traced. For example, if one of your overall goals was to increase community engagement, then you would set some objectives such as the following:

- Increase attendance at community events by 15% within the forthcoming quarter.
- Establish collaborative relationships with three local entities within the coming six-month period.
- Increase social media engagement likes, shares, comments by 20% within the next three months.
- Volunteer at least 100 hours of community service over the next year.

These give you a clearer trajectory toward your goal. Each objective is specific and measurable, enabling you to follow through on your progress and make necessary adjustments. It is important to note that these are not mere numbers; they are people, and they are actual lives affected. For example, 15% more people showing up to community events would translate into more people encountering the love of Christ and finding a place of belonging within their church community.

The "time-bound" dimension of SMART goals: establishing dates of completion creates a sense of urgency and responsibility, thereby preventing projects from lingering on and never being complete. Unless dates are established, many goals are simply never reached. Realistic time estimations enable the proper apportioning of resources and progress monitoring.

Apart from quantitative goals, there is also a need to set qualitative goals in terms of spiritual impact. These may involve:

- Increase the number of professions of faith publicly in Christ.
- Improve a sense of community and belonging in the church.
- Grow people in spiritual maturity within the church.
- Get more people involved in serving others.

While these goals are more difficult to quantify, they are no less important. You can track progress through anecdotal evidence, member testimonies, and qualitative feedback surveys. These qualitative measures give a more rich, holistic view of the impact of your outreach efforts. They shift the focus from simply counting heads to genuinely assessing the transformative power of your ministry. Remember that success lies in numbers, lives changed, and hearts transformed.

Setting measurable goals and objectives should be a team effort of your church's key leaders and members. In this way, better understanding and acceptance fosters ownership and commitment to such goals. Third, your goals need to be regularly reviewed and revised. The world is not standing still, and neither should your outreach plan. What was effective last year may not be this year. Regular evaluation allows for necessary adjustments to keep your plan relevant and workable.

Consider using a goal-setting framework like the OKR (Objectives and Key Results) method. This structured approach involves defining a clear objective and then identifying three to five key results to measure progress. Example:

Objective: Build better relationships with local organizations through increased community engagement.

Key Results:

1. *By December 31st, our organization will partner with three local non-profit organizations on joint community projects. 2. By July 1st, we will increase participation in our annual community picnic by 20%.*
2. *By the end of the year, host at least four community outreach events, each attended by at least 50 people.*
3. *Establish three volunteer partnerships with local businesses to support our community service programs by September 1st.*
4. *Increase positive mentions of our church on local social media platforms by 15% by December 31st.*

This detailed approach provides a clear, measurable pathway to achieving your objective. It allows for focused efforts and accurate tracking of progress. Remember to celebrate milestones along the way, encouraging your team and reinforcing the positive impact of your actions. Celebrate the achievement of numerical goals and the stories of lives touched and transformed. This positive reinforcement strengthens morale and ensures the sustainability of your outreach efforts.

Integrate prayer into every aspect of goal setting and implementation. Seek God's guidance in selecting your objectives, allocating resources, and evaluating results. Prayer is not just an additional activity but the very foundation on which your entire outreach plan should be based. In placing your trust in God, you will find wisdom, strength, and the confidence that your efforts, imperfect as they may be, are part of His larger, divine purpose. The results are not always immediate. Still, with faithful prayer and hard work, you will see His hand at building His Kingdom through your church's outreach initiatives.

Creating a Budget and Allocating Resources

Building a sustainable outreach plan requires a realistic budget and wise use of resources. It's not just about throwing money at the problem; it's about strategic investment with maximum spiritual return. Start by carefully assessing your church's current financial situation. Transparency is key. Engage your church's economic leadership, a finance committee, or board members in this process. Discuss openly the resources and liabilities that exist and possible funding streams. Be transparent about limitations; naming constraints is often the first step to making good decisions. A thorough financial review should detail past giving patterns, find recurring expenses, and project future income based on trends in the past and expected growth. Set up an inclusive financial statement detailing your income streams (through tithes, offerings, special events, grants, etc.) and expenditures that include rent, utilities, employee salaries, program expenses, marketing costs, etc. You get a snapshot of how the church is doing, moneywise. This fiscal openness instills trust into the congregation that they're making responsible stewardship over their gifts.

Once you know what you can count on, you may construct your outreach budget. A detailed document should list each outreach initiative and its associated costs. For example, a youth group mission trip will require funding for transportation, accommodation, meals, and activity expenses. A community event might require venue rental, marketing materials, and entertainment costs. An online marketing campaign will involve website design or maintenance costs, social media advertising, or email marketing services. Be specific; avoid vague estimations. The more precise your budget, the more effective your resource allocation will be.

Building a sustainable outreach program is a marathon, not a sprint. Therefore, avoid overextending yourselves financially. Prioritize initiatives that align directly with your church's mission and vision. It's better to invest strategically in fewer, well-executed programs than to spread resources thinly across numerous initiatives that lack focus and impact. For instance, if your church focuses on involvement within the community, consider organizing an event for a local food bank or performing a clean-up in your community over a large-scale conference that may over-extend the church. Consider additional funding methods apart from the regular tithes and offerings, including grants, fundraising events, and partnering businesses that share values similar to your church. Grants from foundations or organizations that support religious or charitable work can significantly augment your outreach budget. Fundraising events, such as bake sales, car washes, or concerts, can raise extra funds while involving the congregation and encouraging community involvement. Partnerships with local businesses can also provide several resources, such as in-kind donations or advertising support, without significant financial outlay.

Apportion resources equitably. Every ministry in your church should have the opportunity to express its needs and provide some justification for its budget request. This means involving a representative of the different ministries in allocating the budget. In this way, it helps to share the responsibility among all, and no single ministry is left out. Transparency in this process helps avoid misunderstandings and fosters a spirit of partnership and cooperation. Establish clear criteria for evaluating budget requests based on factors such as alignment with the church's mission, potential impact, and cost-effectiveness. This ensures objective and equitable allocation of limited resources.

Your outreach isn't solely measured by monetary success. While a healthy budget is essential, it's critical to remember that the ultimate goal is spiritual growth and transformation. Therefore, include non-monetary resources in your planning. These may consist of volunteer time, prayer support, and the talents and skills of your congregation members. Many people have a wealth of knowledge and experience that can be invaluable to your outreach efforts. Identifying and leveraging these resources can significantly minimize the financial load and engage more of your community. A talented graphic designer within your congregation could provide effective marketing materials, while a skilled musician might spearhead a benefit concert.

The sustainability of your initiative requires periodic budget and resource allocation evaluation. Keep close track of expenses against the planned budget. If variances occur, understand why and make changes where needed. This must be a transparent process with your church's financial leaders. Regular review helps maintain financial responsibility and provides valuable insights into the effectiveness of your outreach strategies. For instance, if a particular outreach initiative proves ineffective despite sufficient funding, it might be time to reconsider its allocation of resources or even its continuation.

Beyond financial resources, consider the allocation of human resources. This includes the time, talents, and skills of your church members. Develop a method for recruiting, training, and managing volunteers involved in your outreach efforts. This will help ensure that volunteer management effectively facilitates your work's success. Clearly define roles and responsibilities for volunteers, provide them with necessary training, and recognize and value their contributions. Regular opportunities for communication and feedback will further keep them motivated. Properly trained and supported volunteers are invaluable assets that can significantly extend the reach of your outreach programs.

Prayer should lead and undergird all aspects of your budgeting and resource allocation. Seek God's wisdom in making financial decisions, trust in His provision, and be open to His guidance in unexpected opportunities. Pray for wise stewardship of the resources entrusted to your church. Pray for the hearts and minds of those who will be served through your outreach efforts and the volunteers who give their time and talents to expand the Kingdom of God. Your budgetary planning and resource allocation are not just financial exercises but acts of faith and worship. In this critical area, coming before God for guidance ensures that your efforts align with His will and that your outreach plan is based on love and compassion. It combines financial prudence with spiritual sensitivity and will lay the foundation for a sustainable and effective outreach strategy.

Building a Strong Marketing Team

Building a strong marketing team is not just about finding people to manage social media accounts or design flyers. It's about assembling a group of individuals who share the passion of spreading the Gospel and possess complementary diverse skills. This calls for being thoughtful and prayerful in approach, knowing each brings unique gifts from God. The shared vision and purpose are the foundation of any successful church marketing team. Before recruiting, ensure your church leadership and marketing committee have a clear idea of what they want to achieve. What exactly are you trying to accomplish? Are you trying to increase church attendance, expand your community outreach, or boost online engagement? A well-defined vision will serve as a compass, guiding your team's efforts and ensuring everyone is working towards a common objective. Transparency is paramount; communicate your church's mission, values, and marketing objectives to potential volunteers.

Recruitment should be an intentional and inclusive process. Don't limit your search to those already highly involved in the church. Seek out individuals from diverse backgrounds and with varying skill sets. Consider developing a thorough volunteer profile that outlines the key responsibilities and skills needed for various positions in the marketing team. This will be a great tool in attracting the right candidates and an exact expectation-setting tool. Use multiple means of recruitment. Make announcements during church services, promote volunteer opportunities through your website and social media platforms, and consider partnering with local community organizations to reach a wider pool of potential volunteers. Remember to highlight the spiritual rewards of serving on the marketing team. Emphasize the opportunity to use their talents to further God's kingdom and share the transformative message of Christ.

Once you've identified potential candidates, the interview process is key. Please find out more about their technical abilities. Question them about their spiritual maturity, commitment to the church's mission, and even how they view marketing within the ministry. Provide open-ended questions to allow candidates to express their passion and describe how their skills will add value to the team's success. Look for technical skills, a collaborative spirit, a desire to learn, and a commitment to serving others. In your interviews, present them with hypothetical situations they may face and how they would handle them. For instance, "How would you handle negative comments on our social media pages?" or "How would you work with a team member with a different approach to a project?" These questions show problem-solving skills and team spirit, some essential characteristics a good team player will possess. Training is among the most important things to build within a marketing team. Remember, just because people are in your church doesn't mean they know how to run social media, make graphics, or create email campaigns. Take the time and effort to train them in everything they need to know. Consider workshops or training sessions on various activities: social media marketing, graphic design, content creation, email marketing, and website management. Complement face-to-face training with online tutorials and webinars. Provide mentors for the new volunteers by assigning them to an experienced team member who can give them advice and assistance.

This mentorship program ensures that new volunteers are quickly integrated into the team, receive immediate help when necessary, and learn best practices from others with more experience. A mentorship will help develop a culture of collaboration and can make your team much more effective. Ongoing training is equally important. The digital landscape changes constantly, so regular updates and skill-building sessions are essential to keep your team at the forefront of effective marketing strategies. Encourage team members to attend conferences or webinars related to church marketing. Establish a system for sharing the team's best practices and new technologies, perhaps through regular meetings or online forums.

Provide opportunities for continuing education on new social media platforms, best practices in email marketing, and SEO optimization. This continued learning maintains the team's skills and conveys your professional and spiritual growth interest. Beyond the technical skills, impress the spiritual formation of your team members. Regular prayer and devotional time, in addition to the usual team meetings, help reinforce the common spiritual bond of the team. Allow open communication and an atmosphere where team members can easily share their faith and struggles.

Lead team discussions of the biblical basis for marketing and outreach, discussing the responsibility of sharing the Gospel with accuracy and sensitivity. Remember, your team is not just running a marketing campaign; they are representatives of Christ, and their spiritual lives will affect how well they function. Create a focused communication plan within the team's internal workings. Schedule regular meeting times, project management tools, and accessibility to resources and information updates. This will eliminate confusion, reduce friction, and ensure everyone is on the same page. Consider using a project management platform, such as Asana or Trello, to track activities and due dates for various marketing projects. Regular check-ins and weekly or bi-weekly team meetings are crucial for encouraging communication and proactively working through challenges.

Clearly define roles and responsibilities among team members to ensure accountability and avoid duplication of efforts. An adequately organized communication setup reduces misunderstandings and disarray, making it easy to have a smooth work process with better collaboration. Delegate responsibilities efficiently. Be mindful of the burden on any one person; different members have different capabilities and time to commit. It requires a good understanding of each person's strengths and passions. By matching tasks to skills, you ensure everyone feels valued, increases their sense of ownership, and contributes effectively. Regularly evaluate the team's performance, not just measurable outcomes but also the team dynamics and individual contributions. Constructive feedback is key to team growth. Celebrate successes and acknowledge individual contributions to maintain morale and motivate continued service.

Regularly assess and adjust your team's structure, ensuring it remains aligned with the church's evolving needs and goals. This flexible approach allows for adaptation to new challenges and opportunities. Building a strong marketing team is a long-term investment. It requires ongoing nurturing, training, and support. By fostering a culture of collaboration, mutual respect, and shared faith, you can create a team that effectively communicates the Gospel and strengthens community bonds within your church.

This holistic approach will balance spiritual formation with technical training and create a very convenient and deeply fulfilling ministry experience for all involved. Keep in mind that the true measure of your team's success is not necessarily the number of likes or shares but rather the number of lives that were transformed by the love of Christ.

Establishing a System for Monitoring and Evaluation

It would be best to establish a robust mechanism for monitoring and evaluating your child for sustainable growth. It is not just a question of launching some initiatives and hoping for the best. We must prayerfully and strategically follow up, analyze our results, and change our strategies accordingly. This is responsible stewardship- to ensure that the resources entrusted to us, such as time, talent, and finances, are used effectively to advance God's kingdom. This is not about the number of successes but rather about understanding qualitatively how our efforts touch the lives of individuals and the community.

The first step in establishing this monitoring and evaluation system is defining key performance indicators (KPIs). What tangible and intangible outcomes are you seeking? Are you looking to increase attendance at your services? Are you hoping to see more people actively involved in small groups or serving ministries? Do you want to see a growth in baptisms or professions of faith? These are all good metrics but shouldn't be the only ones.

In addition to numbers, take count with some qualitative measures: Does a person feel welcome in and find a supportive community in the church? Do people feel like they have a better sense of their relationship with God due to your outreach? Can spiritual transformation be evidenced within the people's lives in which you are reaching? The indicators listed above, by no means exhaustive, speak often to a depth not discovered merely by evaluating through statistics alone. This requires listening to your congregation and collecting information through surveys, interviews, and informal conversations.

Developing a comprehensive data collection system is essential. This might involve utilizing church management software to track attendance, membership, and giving. It could also create simple online surveys to gather feedback on specific events or initiatives. Remember, the goal isn't to overwhelm people with data collection but to gather relevant information that informs future strategies. Please keep it simple and focus on the most crucial information to understand your progress.

Regular reporting is key. Set up periodic meetings with your church's leadership and marketing team to discuss the results gathered. It's not just about giving numbers; it's a time of thoughtful discussion and prayerful reflection. Ask yourself these questions: What are we learning from the data? Where are we seeing success, and where are we falling short? What adjustments might we make to be even more effective? These meetings should be times of problem-solving together and planning strategies under the Holy Spirit's guidance.

Be transparent: Share through the congregation—not a report of numbers but a testimony to the work of God. Highlight successes and challenges with humility, recognizing that outreach is an ongoing faith journey. This creates a sense of shared responsibility and invites all to participate in ongoing improvement.

In addition to regular reporting, periodic deeper reviews should be done. This could include focus groups of targeted segments of your congregation or community to delve deeper into their experiences with your outreach. Consider post-program surveys to assess the quality of programs. These more comprehensive evaluations can provide rich qualitative data to complement regular reporting.

Your monitoring and evaluation system shouldn't operate in a vacuum. It should be linked to your outreach plan and the church's mission and vision. All your efforts should align with the core values of your faith community and be oriented toward fulfilling your spiritual purpose. The goal is not simply to maximize attendance or engagement but to see lives transformed by the power of the Gospel. This requires constant reflection on how your efforts contribute to the growth of individuals' spiritual lives and the building of a vibrant faith community.

Let's explore some practical examples to illustrate these principles. Imagine a church launching a new small group ministry. Their KPI might include the number of new small groups formed, the average attendance per group, and participant feedback regarding their experience. They might use a simple signup sheet to track participation and a brief online survey after each session to gather input. Regular reporting at staff meetings would allow them to identify successful strategies and address challenges promptly. A periodic focus group could provide deeper qualitative insights into the participants' spiritual journeys and the effectiveness of group leaders. This would create a comprehensive approach whereby the church can make data-driven adjustments to enhance the overall impact of their small group ministry.

Consider another example: a church implementing a new social media strategy. Their KPIs might include follower growth, website traffic originating from social media, and levels of engagement, such as likes, shares, and comments. They might use the analytics platforms built into most social media to track the data and inform content strategy. Every once in a while, the team will hold A/B testing to understand which type of posting style works best. Data-driven, this aids their attempt to optimize social media impact for the highest outcomes for sharing the message of salvation. Another good example may be a church leading community outreach events like offering meal programs or leading cleaning neighborhoods. Some example KPIs for them may include how many people are served, the level of community involvement, and direct feedback from participants and volunteers. Attendance could be quantified using sign-in sheets, and input could be collected using short surveys or casual discussions. Based on this data, the church should know how well the event was pulled off and alter plans to keep outreach programs fresh and relevant.

The key to effective monitoring and evaluation is not just the data itself but how you prayerfully interpret and apply it. Be flexible and adapt to the fact that your strategies will change with time. It is an ongoing process of learning, refinement, and growth. Remember that God is in control and your efforts through prayer and a commitment to His purpose bear fruit in His time. The success of your outreach efforts is to be measured not simply by the numbers but by the transformation of hearts and lives to the glory of God.

It is also essential to recognize that there are limitations. The collection of data is very time-consuming and requires specific people or volunteers. Much of the data will not easily be quantifiable, particularly the qualitative aspects of spiritual transformation. Then again, there is the danger of misinterpreting the data, thus arriving at a faulty conclusion. An essential ingredient in the whole system is regularly seeking guidance through the Holy Spirit. God's wisdom will give perspective to the interpretation of data and allow the making of wise decisions in His will.

Your monitoring and evaluation system should not be a burden but a helpful tool. Please keep it simple, focused, and relevant to your goals. Use technology and resources wisely, and most importantly, always approach this process with humility, seeking God's guidance and trusting in His power to transform lives. By establishing a well-organized monitoring and evaluation system regarding your church's outreach plan, you will be assured of the effectiveness and sustainability of the effort and even glorifying God. The emphasis is on effectively communicating the Gospel and changing lives, where people are drawn closer into a relationship with Christ.

Adapting Your Plan for Long-term Success

Adapting your outreach plan isn't a one-time event; it's an ongoing process of refinement and recalibration. Think of it as shepherding a flock—you constantly adjust your approach based on the sheep's needs and responses. Similarly, your church's outreach requires consistent attention and adaptation to remain practical and relevant in a constantly changing world. The key lies in actively listening to the Holy Spirit's guidance and responding to feedback from your community and the broader world.

One key component of adaptation is the ongoing review of data being collected through your monitoring and evaluation system. Numbers are not everything. Quantitative measures such as the number of attendees hit on the website and social media activity are all essential to understanding in concert with qualitative data. Is the audience profoundly engaging in the message? Are lives being transformed? Are new relationships with Christ being formed? Are your members growing in their faith? These questions, though, reveal the effectiveness of your outreach. Go beyond the numbers to explore some stories. Interviews, surveys, or focus groups will provide additional feedback that is much richer in texture. Consider an example: A church has created a dynamic social media effort to reach young adults. Engagements were high early on- many likes, shares, and comments. However, after a few months, the church noticed the number of attendees to events and services was decreasing. In follow-up interviews, they found out that though the online content was relatable, many young adults were apprehensive about attending physical events due to social anxiety or not finding a welcoming atmosphere. These responses have highlighted a serious gap between online engagement and real-world participation. The church then accommodated this by making small, cozy places for gathering and using icebreaker activities to make new people feel their comfort zone. This little accommodation made a massive difference in attendance and community building.

The other important accommodation area involves keeping up with changes and cultural trends. What worked for your community five years ago may not work today. In particular, the digital world moves: New platforms pop up, algorithms change, and users' use changes. Your outreach strategy should change along with them to effectively convey your message to your target audience. Perhaps a specific social media platform is losing popularity, and you need to reallocate your resources to a more effective channel. A new technological tool can help you reach a wider audience or streamline your processes. This requires continuous learning and a willingness to experiment with new approaches.

Adaptability also involves responding to unexpected events. A natural disaster, a community crisis, or a global pandemic can dramatically affect your outreach work. Your plan must be flexible enough to shift and adapt to these situations. Perhaps you need to shift resources to immediate relief efforts or change how you communicate to speak to your community's fears or concerns in a challenging time. For instance, during the COVID-19 pandemic, many churches seamlessly transitioned to fully online services and outreach programs. Others transitioned to offering socially distanced outdoor services or small group gatherings. The key factor was adaptability—reimagining and repurposing what they had for the moment's needs.

Effective adaptation also involves seeking outside input. Don't be afraid to ask for frank opinions from people other than your friends. Invite community leaders, representatives of different churches, or even non-believers to give their take on your outreach efforts. This outside perspective will allow you to identify blind spots or areas for improvement that you may not have seen yourself. It's essential to be open to constructive criticism, understanding that it's not an attack but a rich learning opportunity. You might form an advisory board with diverse backgrounds and experiences to provide much-valued insights into your ever-changing community needs and dynamics.

Adaptation involves constant assessment of your goals and objectives. Is the right audience still being reached? Is the message clear? Do the activities align with the overall mission and vision of the church? Revisiting these basic questions regularly helps keep an outreach plan focused and purposeful. It may mean scaling back on specific initiatives that prove ineffective and refocusing your resources on those that yield better results. This may involve hard choices, but honest self-assessment is essential to long-term sustainability.

Another key component of a sustainable outreach plan is creating a culture of continuous learning within your church. This includes training and developing your team with all the skills and knowledge necessary to manage and adapt your outreach efforts. Regular team meetings, workshops, and conferences can provide opportunities for sharing best practices, discussing challenges, and exploring new approaches. It is also essential to foster a spirit of experimentation and innovation within your team, encouraging them to try new things and learn from successes and failures.

Perhaps most importantly, remember to pray for guidance throughout the entire process of adaptation. Seek God's wisdom and direction in every decision, relying on His strength to navigate the inevitable challenges and uncertainties. Trust that He is working through your efforts, using your church to reach His people. This continued reliance on God's leading will make your outreach plan more effective, your faith more substantial, and your relationship with Him deeper. The bottom line for success is numerical growth and spiritual transformation-lives changed, hearts touched, and souls drawn closer to Jesus Christ. You can have a reproducible outreach plan that gives glory to God and blesses your community generation after generation. Pray consistently, evaluate in a dedicated manner, and change at will. Let your flexibility mirror God's ever-evolving, always-there, and constantly adjusting to human needs. Let us not forget that God's love is not static but dynamic, changing with the world's needs, and our outreach must be equally dynamic.

Chapter 6

Storytelling for Impact

The Power of Testimonies and Personal Stories

The power of a well-told story is simply unsurpassed. It crosses cultural barriers, reaches deep into emotions, and has a lasting effect that surpasses mere information transfer. This power is exponentially multiplied when applied to church outreach as it affords a unique avenue to present the changing message of the Gospel in a manner that touches hearts and minds. For that matter, testimonies and personal stories are the most valuable means. They humanize this message and make it relatable and believable. They become concrete evidence of God's work, showing His power and faithfulness in life situations. When we stop speaking about abstract theological terms and start sharing the lives of people touched by God, we create a powerful connection with our audience.

Consider the power of a simple testimony given during a church service: the person shares how he struggled with addiction, how he was desperate, and how he met God one day, quite unexpectedly-which led to his recovery and faith. This raw, unfiltered narrative speaks volumes more than any carefully crafted sermon could about the authenticity of faith and its power to heal and transform even the most broken lives. It brings hope to others facing similar adversities, reminding them they are not alone and redemption is possible. It's not just about the words but the vulnerable honesty and the palpable presence of God's grace inside the story.

The truth of this principle can spill outside the church walls. In this digital age, personal stories can be shared across many platforms-from social media posts and website testimonials to engaging videos and podcasts. A short video showcasing a young person's journey to faith, their struggles with doubt, and ultimate acceptance of God's love can reach a vast audience, inspiring others to consider their relationship with faith. Similarly, a blog post detailing a family's experience overcoming a challenging life event through prayer and unwavering faith can create a powerful connection with readers. This is powerful marketing, but it's done with integrity, grounded in truth, and designed to inspire, not merely promote.

Testimonials and personal stories are only effective if they are real. They need to be heartfelt expressions of faith, not clever marketing ploys. The stories should be relevant to universal struggle, hope, and transformation. They also need to point to the character and love of God through active involvement in individuals' lives. They need powerful stories that will ring true to the human experience.

To make these stories as impactful as possible, here are a few things to consider:

- Diverse stories: Collect testimonials from people of various ages, backgrounds, and experiences. It creates this tapestry of voices, each speaking to the wide-reaching nature of God's love and grace. Inclusivity ensures the audience sees themselves reflected in the stories.

- Focus on transformation: Describe how faith has transformed individuals' lives. Explain how the faith has brought about good changes in personal relationships, career, emotional stability, and spiritual development. These are strong examples to prove a relationship with God is very effective.

- Permission and privacy: Always get an individual's consent before sharing their story. Respect their privacy and handle sensitive information with care. This is a matter of respect and ensuring that those offering their stories feel secure in their willingness to share.

- Devise engaging narratives: Retain authenticity but shape the stories to create a compelling narrative. This may be done by identifying a clear beginning, middle, and end. The structure will help engage the audience. It's not a matter of manipulation but sound storytelling principles.

- Engage through visuals: Use images or videos corresponding to the stories to enhance their effect. A photo of a person with their testimony adds a human touch, making them more relatable.

- Utilize various media channels: Share the stories across multiple platforms to reach a broader audience. Adapt the stories to suit each platform, adjusting the length, style, and format as necessary. If it's a podcast, ensure the voice is relatable and comforting. If it's a short social media post, make it concise and impactful.

- Create opportunities for interaction: Ask questions, begin discussions, or allow others to share their experiences to involve the audience. This opens up the space for community and connection, building a space for fellowship.

- Measure impact: While avoiding numeric metrics alone, one may measure the effect of shared stories by monitoring engagement, feedback, and further requests for information. This refines outreach strategies to better connect with people.

Beyond personal testimony, consider the impact of case studies demonstrating how ministry initiatives have been effectively carried out. For example, a case study might show how a small church used social media to reach a particular segment of its community, giving attention to the prayerful process of formulating the strategy and its positive outcomes regarding spiritual growth within the community rather than numerical metrics. Another case study might outline the community outreach program a church was involved in, which created a real-life positive change in the lives of individual people and families.

These case studies inspire and provide practical examples that other churches can learn from and contextualize in their situations. They demonstrate faith-based marketing strategies that work: how a church can connect better with the community in which it finds itself and share the Gospel message and its positive influence with a lost world. These successes are shared as stories of what can be accomplished through faith, prayer, and dedication to the mission.

The intentional and strategic use of testimonies to make this case study more impactful, consider adding images or videos racing authenticity, focusing on transformation, and using various media channels, churches can leverage compelling storytelling to more deeply relate with their audiences- in whatever way they may look- so spiritual growth and a strong community can be built. It means remembering that it is not about getting people to the church but inviting them into a relationship with God, where they will experience His love, grace, and power. It requires honesty, vulnerability, and deep respect for those sharing their stories. The resulting impact on lives and communities will show God at work.

Crafting Compelling Case Studies

Practical case studies require a recitation of events and a narrative arc that engages an audience and can be remembered. This is to inform, inspire, and encourage others toward similar journeys of faith and service. We need to go beyond dry statistics and technical details, bringing life into the data by focusing on the human element: those whose lives were changed and communities that were empowered.

Consider a church that initiated a community garden project. An essential case study would say, "The garden supplied fresh produce to needy families." But a more engaging story would go deeper. It would introduce Sarah, a single mother who struggled to feed her children, whose life was significantly impacted by the consistent access to nutritious vegetables. The story would weave in the challenges faced- securing land, overcoming unexpected weather, dealing with volunteer shortages- showcasing the perseverance and faith of the church members involved. It would highlight the community spirit fostered through shared labor and the unexpected friendships that blossomed. It would describe the tangible impact on Sarah's family: how the garden provided food and instilled a sense of hope and dignity. The case study would then connect this specific experience to the broader vision of the church's outreach, showing how a relatively simple initiative had far-reaching consequences, reaching beyond physical needs into spiritual and emotional well-being.

Another example could be a church's successful youth mentorship program. Rather than stating how many participated and how much their grades improved, a compelling case study would tell the story of individuals. Perhaps it includes a story of Michael, an at-risk youth who took advantage of the program. It highlights his path from a confused, somewhat isolated young person to an outwardly confident, responsible adult. The narrative would touch upon the impacts of Pastor John and all the others who invested in making Michael more fully himself. It would fill in the details of some specific challenges overcome, struggles faced, and victories celebrated by real people, showing how the program worked through their stories. The case study will further analyze the program's structure, methodology, and challenges, offering practical insights to other churches willing to consider a similar initiative. Importantly, it would spell out the underlying spiritual principles driving the program and highlight how the mentors' faith played a crucial role in their success.

Likewise, a church's outreach to the homeless could be shown by statistics on the meals served or shelter provided and in telling a series of poignant stories. Each story would have a specific individual as its main character, tracing his journey from despair to hope. We met Maria, who had found comfort and acceptance among the church people, who discovered needs being met within the church and the understanding and love that promoted spiritual development. Therefore, Her story would represent the very essence of that church's ministry, including the holistic approach to the physical and spiritual needs of those in need. The case study may involve interviews with Maria, volunteers, and the church's leadership that further enhance the story and provide a multi-dimensional perspective and testimony to the transformation inspired by faith-based service. It could analyze this program's logistic and financial aspects while always keeping its core human.

These case studies must be elaborately developed to create maximum effect. Note the following elements below:

- Clear Narrative Arc: Every story needs a clear, compelling narrative arc with a clear beginning, rising action, climax, and resolution to keep the reader involved and concerned about the outcome.
- Focus on Transformation: Emphasis should be made on the positive changes in the lives of the individuals and communities involved. Give examples of spiritual growth, improved relationships, or other increased well-being.
- Data Integration: Even as the human element remains the focus, relevant data must be integrated into the story. This may include statistics on participation, impact, or growth, which would thus provide quantifiable proof of the initiative's success. The data must always

complement the storytelling and not overshadow the human element.

- Visual Appeal: Consider adding images or videos to make this case study more impactful. Visuals make the stories more relatable and, thus, more memorable.

- Lessons Learned: Ultimately, conclude each case study with lessons learned and generalizable insights that can prove helpful for other churches also considering similar initiatives. Allow readers to apply the lessons learned in their contexts and be able to replicate successful strategies.

- Authenticity and Vulnerability: Honesty is crucial. Acknowledge challenges faced and lessons learned, showcasing both successes and failures. This will add credibility and demonstrate the genuine nature of the ministry's efforts. Share stories of setbacks and how faith helped overcome them, reminding the readers that ministry is not always smooth sailing.

- Call to Action: Conclude with a specific call to action, encouraging readers to participate in similar community activities. This would, in turn, provide an avenue for putting their faith into action and helping make a difference in people's lives.

By crafting compelling case studies that showcase the transformative power of faith-based initiatives, churches can inspire and motivate others to embark on similar service journeys. These stories will show the fruit of their outreach programs and foster a sense of hope, possibility, and shared purpose within the broader Christian community. Remember that the aim is to inspire a zeal for transformative ministry. If we tell these stories well, we can persuade others to join God's work of expanding His kingdom and radically touching lives. The power of a well-told story, rooted in faith and authentic experience, is a force that can change the world.

Using Visuals to Enhance Storytelling

Building on the power of compelling narratives, we will now explore the crucial role of visuals in amplifying your church's storytelling. While words paint a picture, visuals bring that picture to vibrant life, making your message unforgettable and deeply resonant with your audience. In a world saturated with information, capturing attention requires more than just well-crafted text; it demands a multi-sensory experience. Imagine a strong photograph of a community service project: faces of volunteers aglow with happiness and compassion or authentic smiles from those whose lives have been touched. There's no way the most articulate written description could have that effect. Effective use of visuals is not just decoration; it's a strategic element in communicating your message. It's about choosing images and videos that resonate with your audience's feelings, reinforcing the narrative, and deepening their understanding of your church. A well-chosen visual can sometimes say what words often cannot-touching complex emotions and experiences. Consider the difference between reading about the missionary's experience in a remote village and the photograph of them interacting with the villagers, faces aglow with authenticity and shared humanity. The image brings an instant emotional resonance across languages and cultures.

We now get to some practical considerations for integrating visuals into your storytelling. First, consider the audience. Who is your audience? What sort of imagery will connect most powerfully with these members? A younger crowd will appreciate more dynamic, pulsating videos and catch-your-eye social media graphics; an older demographic perhaps favors more classic photographic images. Knowing the audience's preference helps to downselect visuals that genuinely connect and will not alienate potential members. Knowing your target audience will inform every element, from style and tone to color palette and overall aesthetic.

The quality of your visuals matters immensely. Avoid blurry, poorly lit, or unprofessional-looking images. Invest in high-quality photography and videography, or collaborate with skilled volunteers who can capture impactful visuals. A high-resolution image is beautiful and a sign of care and professionalism that speaks to the credibility and trust your church inspires. This attention to detail shows respect for your audience and communicates that your ministry values quality in all aspects of its communication. Remember, visuals communicate your church's values and commitment to excellence.

The type of visuals you use also makes your message compelling. Photographs are versatile and powerful, capturing many emotions and events. Conversely, videos offer a dynamic medium to tell more affluent, comprehensive stories. Think of short video testimonials from individuals whose lives have been impacted by your church's ministries. These personal accounts create a profoundly moving and persuasive narrative with compelling visuals. Consider also using infographics to present data and statistics in a way that is engaging and easy to digest. For example, an infographic on the number of lives your outreach programs have touched or the growth in your congregation over time will go a long way in visually communicating your ministry's impact.

Beyond still images and videos, consider other visual mediums. Other interactive elements, like quizzes and polls over social media, engage your audience and invite interaction. Animated explainer videos will be significant, and they can take very complex information and put it into a concise, engaging format. They can easily explain your church's mission and the values that guide your ministries or even outline the practical steps involved in getting involved with your church's outreach programs. These forms of engaging visual content can help extend your reach and connect with a broader audience, especially those who would instead consume information in a nontextual format.

Once you have chosen your visuals, incorporating them into your storytelling requires thoughtful reflection. Just don't haphazardly throw images into your content. Please make sure the visuals enhance your message and give it more impact, not distract from it. They support your narrative visually to drive in your key points and create emotional depth in the audience, enhancing what words can say. A good comparison might be that a symphony of images, text, and video create an unforgettable experience together. Let's look at some concrete examples. For instance, a successful case study on community outreach might read: Instead of describing what the program does, intersperse photos of volunteers working with the community. Show the smiles, the collaborative efforts, and the tangible results of the program. Pair these images with short video clips of participants sharing their experiences, expressing their gratitude and the positive impact the program has had on their lives. This multi-layered approach to the case study is infinitely more enjoyable and memorable than the textual account alone could ever be. The reader isn't passively absorbing information but instead participating in a moving visual experience that resonates emotionally.

If you have been showcasing the impact of a particular ministry, such as a youth group or food bank, use visuals to demonstrate reach and impact. Include images of children in purposeful activities, faces aglow with happiness and anticipation. For a food bank, there are photographs of volunteers sorting food and distributing it to the pictures of grateful recipients. These will tell a story of human compassion, generosity, and changes through service. Remember to get permission from those in the photograph, especially around people's testimonials.

We can include visuals in many ways, not limited to written content. Consider using visuals in your church services, presentations, and events. A visually rich presentation with great images and video clips can be more engaging and impactful than a PowerPoint presentation with bullet points and text. Use projected images and video clips to complement the message delivered in sermons or testimonies throughout church services. A large screen displaying images in movement can stir emotions, augmenting the spoken word and heightening the spiritual effect of the message.

Always be authentic and transparent in your visual storytelling. Use visuals that are accurate to your church's work and the lives of the people you serve. Avoid overly staged or artificial imagery; strive for authenticity to build trust and credibility with your audience. Authenticity inspires confidence and invites connection, while inauthenticity can undermine credibility and damage your message.

Consider the accessibility of your visuals. Ensure that images and videos are appropriately captioned and described for those with visual impairments. Accessibility is a crucial element of inclusive ministry, demonstrating your commitment to reaching everyone with the message of Christ. Subtitles and alternative text for images are essential elements for inclusivity, ensuring that your visual storytelling reaches the broadest possible audience and that no one is excluded from experiencing the power of your message.

It is both art and science to use visuals effectively. This effort requires a lot of careful planning, strategic selection, and sensitive integration. By mastering this crucial element in storytelling, you can expand your church's message to connect with your audience in even more profound ways and have further-reaching results in the kingdom of God. Investing in high-quality visual content is an investment in the effectiveness of your ministry and its mission to share with all people the transformative love of Christ. In developing your strategies for visual communication, always remember to seek God's guidance so that your actions may align with your church's values and mission to glorify Him in all that you do.

Sharing Stories Across Various Platforms

We start with the power of storytelling, but now we enter into the critical aspect: how to adapt and share those stories on different platforms. The effectiveness of your church's story depends both on the quality of that story and on its presence and resonance in the given medium. A powerful tale ineffectively told falls flat. A simple story that is effectively told can light up hearts and minds. Therefore, strategic platform selection and tailored content are paramount.

Think about the many ways people consume information today. Some like the immediacy of social media, others like the depth a well-penned blog post offers, and others enjoy the personal connection a face-to-face encounter allows. To have the most significant impact, your storytelling needs to transcend the limitations of a single platform; it needs to be fluid, adaptable, and resonant across modern communication.

Let's start with social media. Each platform has its unique character, audience, and way of communication: Facebook, Instagram, Twitter, and TikTok. An extended, reflective story shared on Instagram may be buried in a sea of rapid images and short-form videos. On the other hand, a short, impactful story shared on Facebook may fail to capture the full depth and nuance of the message.

For example, strong visuals will always help on Instagram. Short videos chronicling a mission trip or highlighting the impact of your church's outreach can catch people's attention. Brief, descriptive captions and relevant hashtags can grossly increase the reach of such posts. The secret lies in using visual documentation of the story, bringing out its emotional core with images and videos while complementing it with tiny bits of text that have an effect.

With Facebook allowing longer texts and broad demographic divisions, more storytelling can be allowed. Share longer blog posts or articles adapted from your website, highlighting powerful testimonies or stories of transformation in your church. Always include images and videos within your Facebook posts to break up the text and help retain viewers' attention. Use Facebook groups to foster a deeper connection with your audience by allowing a space for the community to discuss and share the stories shared.

Twitter, being short-form in nature, is a whole different ball game. Your core focus should be constructing small yet powerful tweets, capturing the most relevant moments or pieces of insight from more significant stories. Apply striking hashtags to increase the visibility of your tweets for more viewership. Consider using Twitter threads to expand on particular stories and encourage discussion. The challenge with Twitter lies in boiling complex narratives down into concise and impactful messages without losing their emotional power.

TikTok, the rapidly growing platform of short-form video content, provides an opportunity to showcase your stories dynamically and engagingly. Short, high-energy videos can capture attention and convey the essence of your church's message in a format that aligns perfectly with the platform's style. Consider utilizing trending sounds and challenges to expand your reach organically. Authenticity and humor, when appropriate, are vital to this platform's success.

Beyond social media, your website is the real hub for story distribution. Here, longer-form narratives, articles, and testimonials can be shared. You can create a unique page or section on impactful stories, organizing them thematically for easy access and navigation. Remember, your website should be visually attractive, user-friendly, and easy to navigate.

Email newsletters offer a more direct way to reach your congregation and broader community. Stories curated and disseminated in regular email newsletters ensure the continuity of engagement and foster relationships. Consider personalizing your emails by segmenting your audience based on their interests or demographics. Ensure your storytelling will always be relevant and inspire positive responses with visuals and calls to action strategically placed inside your email content.

Consider the power of printed materials. Church bulletins, brochures, and flyers can still be useful in telling stories, especially to your local community. But remember, design and content have to be eye-catching and relevant to your audience, or they will soon become useless.

Community events are the best opportunities to share stories directly. Organize events where members of your congregation can share their testimonies. Consider inviting guest speakers to share their stories of faith, resilience, and transformation. These face-to-face interactions are significant in creating a sense of community and sharing the transformative power of your faith.

Sharing stories across platforms will provide regularity of presence and an increased connection with your audience. This ongoing engagement cements your church's message, secures relevance, and nurtures a more connected community inside and outside your immediate congregation.

Track your storytelling performance on each platform with an eye on the likes, shares, comments, and website traffic for starters. Observe which stories touch effectively with your audience and which platform creates the most impact. Make further improvements in your strategy so your storytelling is constantly improved, optimized, and effective. However, it would be wrong to base a measure of success purely on measurable metrics. While these metrics stand and provide a compelling way to get insight into metrics, the right impact quantifies life and the firming of faith through lives in your community.

Consider, too, the importance of diverse voices in your storytelling. Ensure that your narratives reflect the diversity within your congregation; avoid homogeneous storytelling. This kind of authenticity and inclusiveness creates a richer experience that your audience can relate to more easily.

Seek feedback from your community. Ask members of your congregation to provide insight into how they are experiencing your storytelling through the various platforms and what works for them. This direct feedback is a real treasure for understanding your efforts' effectiveness and will inform your future storytelling strategies.

Sharing your church's stories across various platforms requires careful planning, strategic adaptation, and ongoing evaluation. Utilizing a multi-platform approach in a manner relevant to each of them, your stories could create a buzz that captures not just the local community but also shares the transforming love of Christ with the big world outside. Now more than ever, the outreach and ministry of a church could be aided by remembering to pray for guidance and wisdom. The power of your storytelling lies not just in the narratives themselves but in the intention and grace with which they are shared.

Ethical Considerations in Storytelling

The last chapter clarified that choosing the right platforms and crafting your church's stories are critical, but it does not stop there. Storytelling happens within a church only when ethical issues become integral to a story-telling policy or initiative. Storytelling—let alone when using real people and their personal stories of faith—involves accuracy, sensitivity, and respect on deep levels. This section begins the exploration of those crucial ethical dimensions.

Accuracy is paramount. When sharing personal testimonies or stories of how God has answered prayer, accurate retelling of those events is essential. Exaggeration, embellishment, and outright fabrication erode trust and can severely damage the credibility of your church's communications. Individuals whose stories are being used should be able to review and approve the story before it is published or distributed. This collaborative approach ensures a story is represented faithfully and void of misinterpretations or distortions. Remember, a goal is to glorify God-not to fictionalize an account for emotional appeal.

Beyond factual accuracy lies the critical aspect of sensitivity. Many stories shared in a church setting involve vulnerable people in personal struggles, challenging life circumstances, or profound spiritual transformations. These individuals have entrusted their experiences to the church community, and treating their stories with the utmost care and sensitivity is very important. Avoid gratuitous details or exploitive elements. Focus on the uplifting aspects of the story while maintaining respect for the privacy and dignity of the individual.

Privacy respect is the bottom line. A prerequisite of consent from any participant for publishing his story must be acquired, mainly if such participants are identifiable. Consent to be given by explicit permission of the person whose story one wants to share should be explicitly expressed. Implied or presumed permission shall not suffice. The client shall know how the story will be used, shared where, and with implications on its potential publishing. This process will protect individuals' privacy and make them feel comfortable and respected.

Please think of the repercussions it may have on his reputation and well-being. Well-intentioned stories may even have hurtful consequences in one way or another. For instance, personal struggles a person has gone through may be sensitive information that might be taken out of context or abused. Always weigh the possible benefits of sharing the story against the potential harm it could cause. If there's a reasonable risk of damage, it's ethically responsible to refrain from sharing the story.

Be cautious. When anonymity is required to maintain the person's privacy, be even more careful to avoid telling their story in a way that reveals their identity. Consider using a pseudonym or changing identifiable details to protect the storyteller but retain the story's message. Remember, the attention should be on glorifying God and uplifting the community, not on the sensationalism of individual experiences.

Consider the implications of storytelling for children and minors. Their vulnerability requires even greater caution and care. Always obtain parental or guardian consent before sharing any story related to a child. The protection of their privacy and well-being should be the utmost priority. Even if a child's story is inspirational, one must respect autonomy and privacy.

Ethical storytelling extends beyond individual stories to encompass broader community narratives. Maintaining accuracy and fairness when presenting your church's history or sharing stories of its impact on the community. Avoid biased or one-sided narratives. Acknowledge challenges or shortcomings and strive for a balanced representation of the church's journey.

Moreover, be mindful of cultural sensitivities. Stories that resonate deeply within one cultural context might be offensive or misunderstood in another. Sensitivity to cultural differences and treating these stories with respect and understanding is essential. Translation and adaptation should be handled with utmost care and respect for the target culture. Always ensure that the story's essence is preserved while accommodating cultural nuances.

Another important consideration is using other religious groups or worldviews. When sharing interactions with individuals of different faith traditions, it is essential to treat these stories with respect and understanding. Generalizations and stereotypes must be avoided. Commonalities and mutual respect will be discussed in detail throughout interfaith dialogues.

Storytelling in a church should never be underestimated. Ethical considerations are not optional guidelines but principles that should permeate every level of your communication strategy. By being sensitive to the need for accuracy, respect for privacy, and awareness of cultural sensitivity, you make sure your stories reflect Christ's love, grace, and compassion, thus building your community and sharing God's transformative power with the world. It is about marketing your church and reflecting God's character in every aspect of your communication. Remember that real impact is born from authenticity, transparency, and deep respect for the human experience. The process of ethical storytelling is ongoing as well. Regularly revisit and refine your approach. Seek feedback from your community to ensure that your efforts ring authentically and do not bring harm where it is least intended. Pray and reflect constantly for guidance on sharing a story, that God's wisdom will be sought in each situation. This will lead to a continuous commitment to ethical principles that will engender trust, strengthen your community, and amplify the transformative power of God's message. It's not just a matter of telling stories; it's sharing the love of Christ in a truthful, respectful, empowering way.

Ethics are not only about preventing harm but also about actively promoting good. Your stories can inspire, uplift, and give hope. By using your storytelling responsibly and with ethics, you can amplify this positive impact, enriching the lives of individuals and strengthening the bonds within your community.

This approach places your church as a beacon of truth, compassion, and integrity, a testament to the transformative power of God's love. The enduring power of your message will not rest solely on its eloquence but on the ethical foundation upon which it is built. Ultimately, the most impactful stories reflect God's glory and His people's unwavering commitment to moral principles.

Chapter 7

Building Relationships Through Events

Planning Meaningful and Engaging Events

Planning meaningful and engaging events is crucial for building relationships within your church and reaching out to the broader community. It's more than just throwing a party; it's about strategically crafting experiences that reflect God's love and draw people closer to Him. This requires careful planning, a deep understanding of your audience, and a commitment to creating a welcoming and inclusive environment. Let's explore the key elements of planning successful church events.

First, identify who your target audience is. For whom are you trying to provide ministry? Are you focusing on young families, adults, senior citizens, or a broader reach? Knowing what interests them, what they need, and what they like helps you design events that genuinely reach them. For example, a youth event can be games, music, and interactive activities, while a senior event would be more about fellowship, inspiring speakers, and comfortable seating. Consider surveys, focus groups, or simply talking with them for helpful insights. Analyzing demographics and the participation patterns in your current congregation will also point out underserved segments so that you can plan specific events to meet their needs. Remember, you want large numbers and to nurture faith while building community.

Now, brainstorm event ideas, thinking broadly. The possibilities are endless. Think about hosting a family fun day with games, crafts, food trucks, or a community concert showcasing local talent. A guest speaker event with a strong message can draw people seeking spiritual insight. A service project, like a community cleanup or food drive, allows for practical outreach and shows God's love in action. For young adults, a social gathering with games and live music may be more in order, while a more formal dinner may be more to the liking of older generations. Also, remember the time of year and any events happening within your community. Do not plan competing events that detract from your church's activities. A well-timed event capitalizes on existing interests within the community and can maximize its impact.

Another critical factor is the location of your event. Choose a venue that is accessible, comfortable, and appropriate to the activity. A hall can be ideal for concerts or family gatherings, while a smaller room will be more effective for Bible studies or prayers. There should be accessibility for people with disabilities, such as ramps, elevators, and seating. The atmosphere where the event will be held is vital to reflect the kind of event and the intended tone one wants to achieve. For example, a relaxed and informal setting may be appropriate for a youth event, while a more formal setting may be needed for a celebratory one.

Hospitality involves creating an enabling atmosphere where relationships can be established. This includes ensuring everyone feels comfortable, accepted, and valued regardless of background, beliefs, or circumstances. Use inclusive language in all promotional material and welcome people warmly on arrival.

Make all activities accessible and enjoyable. Include times when people can get to know one another: icebreakers, small group discussions, mealtimes together. If possible, provide childcare for families with young children. Most importantly, create a caring and grace-filled atmosphere that models God's acceptance of each one of us. This can make a powerful sense of community, a safe and welcoming place where people can explore faith and connect. Remember, genuine hospitality is a manifestation of Christ's love.

When the event is over, the work isn't done. Follow-up is important. Send thank-you notes or emails to those who attended, thanking them for coming and including photos or videos from the event. Inform them via social media or newsletters about forthcoming events and ways to become involved. Follow-up dialogue with those interested in discovering more about your church is critical. This can be done via a phone call, an email, or an invitation to another event. Also, consider providing an opportunity to give feedback, allowing attendees to share their experiences and suggestions for future events. This will help refine your strategies and help your events stay relevant and engaging.

Measuring the success of your events isn't just about counting heads. Besides attendance, an important metric is to focus on the qualitative aspects of the event: Did people feel welcomed and connected? Were there opportunities for spiritual growth? Was the event successful in achieving its intended purpose? Informal surveys, interviews, or response sheets can be used to ascertain what attendees experienced. Observe the interactions and get a feel for the overall atmosphere. Listen for qualitative responses. Sometimes, the most successful events, in terms of legitimate relationships and long-term spiritual results, do not boast the highest attendance numbers.

Planning impactful, interactive events is an ongoing process. Continually assess your approaches, ask for feedback, and be open to changing and improving. Be flexible, open to new ideas, and willing to try different techniques. Prayer and seeking God's guidance should be an integral part of every stage in planning, from conception to post-event evaluation. Remember that each event is a real opportunity to share God's love and build His Kingdom. As you plan events, focus on building relationships, fostering spiritual growth, and extending God's grace to all attendees. Let your events reflect God's welcoming, loving, and transformative character.

To further illustrate, take a church that hosts an annual community Easter egg hunt. They could go beyond the hunt by including a short Easter message, offering complimentary refreshments, and having volunteers available to talk to attendees about the church and its programs. This provides families with a relaxed, enjoyable atmosphere and allows spontaneous sharing of the Gospel message. Or consider a small church that holds monthly potlucks open to the whole community. The atmosphere is friendly and informal, with opportunities for people to interact and get to know each other outside of Sunday services. These events are about attendance, building relationships, and strengthening community bonds. Events could be followed up by the church by sending out newsletters containing pictures from the event and stating further activities, thus making the connections even more potent.

Another example could be a church organizing some community service, such as cleaning up a local park or painting a mural at a community center. This shows that the church is committed to serving the community and gives the congregation opportunities for active work based on their faith. Events like these uplift the community and make the church look good. This realistic approach shows the love of Christ in action, and post-event communications can emphasize the tangible impact of their work.

Leverage technology to extend your events. Streaming events online reach a larger audience. Social media can give events greater exposure, as it allows posting event promotions ahead of time and, after the events, an opportunity for photographs and videos to be posted. Promote engagement within events via interactive components: polls, Q&A, etc., to develop and foster communities. Such technology will strengthen your events, but remember they are tools meant to serve and support actual human interaction along with the Word of Faith. They are tools to enhance, not to dominate, your outreach efforts. By thoughtfully planning and executing your events while remaining grounded in prayer and faith, your church can build strong relationships and grow God's kingdom.

Creating a Welcoming and Inclusive Atmosphere

Creating A truly welcoming and inclusive atmosphere is key to the success of any church event. It's more than just putting up a banner that says "Welcome." It's about creating an atmosphere where people feel real belonging-a sense that they are seen, heard, and valued, regardless of their background, beliefs, or abilities. This involves a multi-dimensional approach, considering both the tangible aspects of the design of the event and the intangible elements of the church culture.

One of the first steps is to ensure physical accessibility. This means making the location of the event readily accessible to persons with disabilities: ramps, elevators, accessible restrooms, and marked pathways. Consider providing assistive listening devices for those with hearing impairments and large-print materials for those with visual impairments. Going beyond the minimum requirements, think proactively about creating a comfortable space for everyone. Adequate seating, appropriate lighting, and a climate-controlled environment are simple yet effective ways to enhance the experience for all attendees.

Inclusiveness, however, goes beyond mere physical accessibility. It extends to the inclusiveness of the programming itself. That would mean no use of language or imagery that could alienate any particular group. This includes using inclusive language: avoiding gendered terms when possible, using person-first language when referring to individuals with disabilities, and being sensitive to culturally specific terminology. Likewise, the sources of music, visuals, and activities should reflect the diversity of the congregation and the community being served. Consider blending musical genres, displaying works from different artists, or planning activities that will be of interest to a number of ages and tastes. This is an event that can help bind everyone together in some way rather than allowing individual differences to separate the audience.

Making people welcome is an act of intentional hospitality. It begins with the greeters and volunteers who open the door for your guests. Training volunteers to be truly welcoming, to smile warmly, and to take the time to learn people's names is key. Clear signage and directions allow visitors to move through the space with ease. A clear area for newcomers or first-time attendees allows them to meet others and ask questions without intimidation. Refreshments and snacks, lighter in nature, prove a small yet effective door into deeper community and knocking down some barriers. Besides the fundamentals, offering something that's gluten-free or vegetarian is a sign of thinking about others and an attempt to be inclusive.

Moving on from the practical standpoint, welcoming requires a rethinking of attitudes. One should go out of their way, consciously, against entrenched assumptions and biases. They are best demonstrated through active promotion and emphasis from church leaders. Stories and testimonies of people from every walk of life within the congregation can really help make this point effectively. Announcements, newsletters, social media, or even the event can be used for this. Opportunities for deep interaction with people from other backgrounds need to be provided. This can be done in the form of icebreakers, discussions in small groups, or meals together where people can be encouraged to talk to each other.

Another important component is active efforts to reduce potential barriers to participation. Financial barriers may lead to an inability to attend events. Offering scholarships or reduced-fee options can make events more accessible to those with limited financial resources. Childcare services can allow parents to participate without worrying about their children. Transportation assistance can be offered to those who lack reliable transportation. These little acts could mean the world of difference to some people and really make it an inclusive setting.

It is not a single event, but rather a continuous process in which effort and attention should be given. It means regularly assessing how well inclusion is working and adjusting the strategies. Sometimes, the collection of feedback from the attendees through surveys, feedback forms, or informal conversations may provide insight into areas that need improvement. This loop of continuous improvement will help keep the church a friendly and inclusive place for everybody.

Consider how technology can help create an inclusive space. Streaming events allows people who cannot be there in person because of illness, location, or disability to participate. Providing closed captioning or translation services opens the event up to a wider audience. Online Q&A components let people who are shy or uncomfortable speaking up in person to interact with the content and community. Yet, remember that technology serves to enhance human connection, not replace it. The heart of people in terms of warmth and real hospitality are still at the core of creating a welcoming atmosphere.

Beyond the practical steps, the heart of a welcoming church is found in the love and acceptance extended to everyone. It reflects God's unconditional love, transcending differences and embracing every individual as a unique and valuable child of God. That is to say, creating space actively for people to share their stories, experiences, and perspectives; nurturing in the community a sense of empathy and understanding. It involves listening to others, rejoicing in diversity, and patience with knowledge in disagreement.

The commitment to love and acceptance needs to permeate the culture of the church rather than be an isolated incident. A welcoming church is where one feels safe to be oneself, where vulnerability is a welcome friend, and all belong. It takes persistent and intentional work on the part of leaders, volunteers, and members alike to create such a church culture. It calls for working deliberately to overcome prejudice, encouraging empathy, and building an accepting culture where everyone shows respect for one another. It is a conscious decision to make space for people to be themselves without judgment or fear.

Creating a friendly and accepting atmosphere is not just about making a pleasant experience; it's about reflecting the love and grace of God to the world. By intentionally seeking to be a place where all people feel welcomed, valued, and loved, the church can be that confident hope and a sure instrument of God's transformational love. This is not a marketing ploy but a reflection of who the church is: a faith community called to love and serve all people. This is a commitment to continuing in prayer, fueled by the love of Christ, through which thriving relationships and kingdom expansion are built. This is a commitment to the inclusive nature of God's love, welcoming all into His table and inviting them to share in the overflow of His grace. It's not optional; it lies at the very core of our faith and mission.

Leveraging Events for Outreach and Connection

Events are, however, more than mere congregation; they are effective instruments of outreach and connectivity. They afford that rare chance to get out of the four-walled Sunday service setting into another environment where people can be much more relaxed and informal. When planned for and executed with great strategy, a church event can catalyze relationships that will last through eternity and extend God's Kingdom. It is just a matter of understanding to whom it is for, orchestrating engaging experiences, and encouraging real connectivity.

Consider your audience: young families, adults, seniors, or a diverse community. Knowing their interests, needs, and preferences will be important in planning an event that will appeal to them. For example, a family-friendly event might include games, crafts, and face painting, while a young adult event could feature a live band, guest speaker, or a casual social gathering. Tailoring the event to your target audience increases the likelihood of attracting them and creating a welcoming atmosphere.

The choice of event type is equally important. The options range from community festivals and concerts to workshops, conferences, and social gatherings. Think outside the box! Perhaps a movie night showcasing faith-based films, a volunteer project serving the community, or a skills-sharing workshop could be appealing. Consider events that reflect the unique strengths and talents within your congregation. A concert could be a powerful draw if your church has gifted musicians. If members have expertise in cooking or gardening, a cooking demonstration or gardening workshop could be attractive options. The possibilities are endless.

Effective promotion is critical to the success of any event. However, all promotion needs to be conducted in service of authenticity and invitation rather than as hard-selling marketing. Utilize both an online and offline, multi-pronged outreach strategy. The usage of social media platforms, including Facebook, Instagram, and TikTok, may reach a wide demographic. Not to say that the use of traditional means-fliers, community center postings, or announcements in local newspapers or newsletters-is unhelpful. Word-of-mouth is still one of the strongest tools; encourage your congregation to spread the word among their friends and family.

It is about creating an environment that is welcoming and inclusive. This is more than comfortable seating and refreshments; it is making people feel welcome and valued.

Ensure the event is accessible to people with disabilities. Ensure there is clear signage and directions. Train volunteers to be welcoming and approachable. Pay attention to the small details; a friendly smile, a warm greeting, or a helping hand can make a significant difference.

Then, on the day of the event itself, plan activities and conversations. Plan activities that spur conversations and connections: icebreaker games, small group discussions, or work projects. Avoid programs with too much structure that make spontaneous interaction difficult. This is relationship-building, not conveying information. Allow time for personal interaction with church members and leaders. Organize small group activities, casual meet-and-greets, or even one-on-one conversations.

Following the event, nurturing the connections made is just as important. Send a thank-you note to those who attended. Follow up with those who expressed interest in learning more about the church. Invite them to upcoming services or events. This follow-up will continue to show your concern and dedication to their relationships. Consider the creation of a post-event survey to garner feedback to make improvements in future events. The data collected can inform your future planning and help you better serve your community.

Remember, an event's success is not necessarily measured by the number of people who attended. Though attendance is important, the ultimate measure of success is how the event impacted the lives of those attending. Did it provide opportunities for spiritual growth? Did it build relationships? Did it help people connect with God and the church community? These qualitative measures are far more significant than quantitative metrics.

Let's consider some practical examples. A church might provide an opportunity for a community service project, such as renovating a park in concert with other civic groups or perhaps cleaning a local beach. This would serve the community and allow the member to interact with the non-believer in a community in a practical expression of the individual's faith. For this purpose, a summertime barbecue might be a light-hearted, casual way to facilitate communication and familiarity among people. Events centered on holidays, such as Christmas concerts or Easter egg hunts, would draw families in and be a fun, festive environment to share the Gospel message.

A church with high musical talent could host a concert with local and nationally recognized Christian artists. This would have the potential to draw big numbers and share the Gospel through music. A creative writing workshop or a photography course could appeal to those with artistic interests, offering a platform for spiritual exploration through creativity. These are just a few examples; the possibilities are limited only by creativity and imagination. The key is to choose events that are authentic to your church's identity and mission and resonate with your community.

Building relationships through events requires a long-term perspective. It is not just a single effort but one that needs persistence. Pacing, reflection, and follow-up must be thoughtful and consistent in depth for any above-average impact. Remember to always pray for guidance and insight as you plan and conduct your event. Seek God's wisdom as you select the right event for your group, promote that event, and foster an atmosphere of genuine relationships. He will bless it and lead you as you take His love to the world.

With great use of technology, your events will go farther and be more effective. Events can be livestreamed to include participants who cannot join in person. An event website or landing page can house necessary information and facilitate event registration. Utilize social media for promotion and to provide live updates during the event. Event management software can streamline registration, communication, and follow-up.

The ultimate objective of your events is not to fill the seats, nor to promote the visibility of your church. It is all about the people getting connected to Christ and having a strong faith community. Center on relationships, sharing the love of Christ, and spiritual development. With this approach, events become the key to seeing the Great Commission fulfilled and God's kingdom expanded.

Also consider feedback. After each event, seek feedback from participants who are members and those who are not. This is extremely important to understand how one can make things better and have an even more compelling future in building relationships and connecting people with Christ. This information may be gathered through surveys, informal conversations, or even social media polls. Be open to constructive criticism and willing to make adjustments based on the feedback you receive. This iterative process will serve to further refine your event planning and assure that your outreach efforts are as impactful as possible.

Prayer is key. From the very inception of a plan through the post-event follow-up, prayer should undergird each step. Pray for the guidance of the Holy Spirit in selecting an appropriate format for the event, wisdom regarding effective promotion, and God's blessing on the event itself. Pray for the hearts of those who attend that they might be open to the message of the Gospel and lasting relationships might be formed. Prayer is the foundation upon which all successful outreach efforts are built. It is a source of strength, guidance, and the turning point that changes lives. By planting your event planning in prayer, you ensure that your efforts are aligned with God's will and that His love is at the heart of everything you do.

Post Event Follow Up and Engagement

The energy of a thriving church event doesn't simply dissipate when the last hymn is sung, or the final prayer is offered. The real impact usually comes through follow-up- in the sustained engagement that nurtures the seeds of connection planted during the event. In this post-event phase, what could have been a series of fleeting encounters gets converted into lasting relationships and, ultimately, furthers the reach of the Gospel. Of course, it's not just sending out an email of thanks; building solid relationships requires mutual faith in each other and a purpose shared between parties.

Successful post-event follow-up demands a multi-pronged approach, utilizing various forms of communication to stay in contact with attendees. Immediately following the event, while fresh, a timely thank-you via email or text message is an absolute must. It's not just a formality but an occasion to express thanks for attending in a heartfelt way and build on positive feelings about the event. A simple heart-to-heart message of recognition of their presence, bringing out a particularly positive aspect from the events, probably a powerful testimony, a moment shared in humor, or a proper connection made along the way.

Beyond the immediate thank-you, a more comprehensive follow-up strategy is in order. A well-crafted e-newsletter, sent within a week of the event, can wrap up the highlights, including photos and videos, if available. This visually engaging content helps to rekindle memories of the event and reignite the positive emotions experienced. The newsletter can also send links to various resources, such as sermon recordings, articles based on the event's theme, or upcoming events/activities at the church. This will keep the buzz alive and encourage further involvement.

Social media sites offer another effective channel for post-event engagement. Sharing photos and videos from the event on platforms such as Facebook, Instagram, and even TikTok using relevant hashtags and encouraging attendees to share their experiences will help create this sense of community and shared identity. Responding to comments and messages on such platforms shows further care for the opinions of those who attended and helps them feel closer. Consider creating a unique hashtag to monitor online conversations about this event and engage with the participants in one place.

The power of personal connection. A phone call or handwritten note expressing appreciation can significantly impact smaller events. This personalized touch demonstrates genuine care and creates a more profound connection than a mass email could ever achieve. Such customized communication can be particularly impactful for those who expressed a specific interest in connecting further or shared a personal story during the event.

On the other hand, it is also not thoroughly followed up with just the direct attendees; one should also include those who showed an interest but did not appear at all. A quick follow-up with regret due to absence, yet the continuing invitation to more events shortly retains belonging and connection. This denotes thoughtfulness and proves the church appreciated their interest even when they were not there.

Besides immediate follow-up, long-term strategies to incorporate attendees into sustainable church groups or ministries must occur continuously within areas that interest them or match their spiritual gifting. Also, inviting them for service opportunities, Bible study, or small group gatherings allows additional times for relating and growth to happen, thus increasing their stick rate in church as their interaction deepens within the group.

Consider creating an email list for event attendees where targeted information about relevant activities, events, and opportunities for engagement can be shared. This will enable regular communication and tailor messages to the group's interests. Inspiring messages, announcements of relevant events, and testimonies from community members are just some regular updates that will keep attendees informed and engaged.

Measuring post-event engagement is not only about numerical metrics. While it's good to track how many are showing up to subsequent events, participating in small groups, or engaging on social media, the objective measure of success needs to be qualitative: Are people growing spiritually? Are relationships deepening? Are new disciples being made? These measures determine whether the post-event outreach and event were genuinely effective. Regularly considering and evaluating the qualitative will pay dividends in refinement and honing for future efforts. In so doing, the follow-up after the event does not lose its vitality in the outreach life of the church. The objective is not simply to attract a crowd for the event but to bring relationships that lead to long-lasting spiritual growth. This period after the event gives ample opportunity to nurture those relationships, offer support, provide encouragement, and give people a better understanding of the love and grace of God. With a thoughtful, all-inclusive follow-up plan, what could be merely one more event for the church will be changed into an actual launching pad for further involvement, spiritual growth, and change. Every touch, every contact, every opportunity to connect is saturated in prayer, appealing to God for His guidance and blessing in each person's spiritual journey.

A holistic approach to post-event follow-up realizes that building takes time and is a process. It is a marathon, not a sprint. It requires patience, perseverance, and a deep commitment to the nurturing of seeds of faith that have been planted. It's about fostering a community where people feel welcome, supported, and helped to grow in faith. This long-term perspective is critical; the initial enthusiasm generated by an event must be nurtured and channeled into lasting and meaningful relationships within the church community.

Feedback is essential. Gather feedback from attendees through questionnaires, focus groups, or informal discussions. Such responses are invaluable in indicating what worked and did not work and what future events could plan for. This feedback loop will continuously improve the execution of coming events and strategies. Through experiences learned and by changing to the needs and preferences that change within the community, the church continues to better its outreach in connecting with people.

This post-event follow-up is not some after-sales marketing exercise in a church context but a ministry opportunity, a chance to extend pastoral care, support members in bad times, and celebrate with them the milestones and victories of their lives. This personal touch sets the church's events apart from those of the world. This is God's love in action, a tangible manifestation of the church's commitment to its members and the community it serves.

Consider the need for further learning and growth even after the event. Make small group discussions, mentorship programs, or opportunities for further study about the event's theme available. This way, such an extended format allows one to plunge deeper into the message and get closer to people with similar interests and experiences. This continued spiritual nurturing ensures that the event's long-term effects continue well past the actual day of the event. As a result of its investment in the spiritual development of its attendees, the church commits itself to its growth in the bonds of community and faith. The follow-up after the event is thus not an end but a new beginning and beginning of lasting relationships, spiritual growth, and extension of God's Kingdom.

Measuring the Success of Events

Not having events that number-based attendance counts usually measure, the perception of how successfully to measure any event in churches needs to change. There needs to be a transition from merely quantity measurements, including the number that attended an event or funds brought into the treasury, to qualities associated with measurement. This, on the one hand, ranges to comprehension and insight that the event affected individual spiritual growth, more substantial relationships amongst the community, and further spread the gospel. This does not demean the value of quantitative data; attendance figures, for instance, outline at least the base level of reach. These numbers in and of themselves will tell only a tiny portion of the story.

Some good ways to measure spiritual impact include follow-up surveys and feedback processes after an event. These mustn't be confined to mere satisfaction ratings. They have to probe into the attendees' personal experiences and reflections. Open-ended questions are essential in this respect. Instead of asking, "Did you enjoy the event?" ask questions like: "What aspect of the event resonated most deeply with you and why?" or "How did the event impact your relationship with God?" or "What specific insights or takeaways do you intend to apply to your daily life?" These questions encourage thoughtful responses that offer valuable insights into the event's spiritual efficacy. Analysis of these can outline trends and themes, showing in greater detail the spiritual effects of the event. Such responses can be further enhanced using qualitative data analysis techniques such as thematic analysis.

Consider administering both pre- and post-event spiritual assessments. These might consist of brief questionnaires on spiritual maturity, faith practice engagement, and feelings toward the church community. Comparing pre- and post-event responses can show the event's contribution to growth in these areas. The design of such assessments needs, however, to be carefully considered to ensure that they appropriately measure the constructs of interest without introducing bias. Collaboration with theologians or spiritual formation experts can be highly beneficial in developing valid and reliable assessment tools.

In addition to individual spiritual growth, community strengthening needs to be assessed. Did the event create a sense of belonging and bonding among the attendees? Does it provide opportunities for the participants to interact meaningfully and build relationships? This may be observed during the event by noting the attendees' level of interaction and participation. The same may also be asked in post-event surveys regarding how much they felt connected with the other attendees and the church community. For instance, some questions can be: "Did you connect with anyone new during the event?" or "How did this event strengthen your sense of belonging within our church community? ". Answers to these will give an insight into the community-building aspect of the event. Another way to measure the success of your church event is to monitor the long-term engagement of attendees. Involvement with the church after the event is more significant compared to before. This may be measured through attendance records, volunteer sign-ups, and participation in other programs at the church.

A marked increase in involvement following the event may suggest that the event was effective in developing a deeper engagement with the community. Again, this requires identifying some obvious metrics through which one could track the longer-term level of engagement and routine analysis of such metrics to establish a judgment about the impact derived from the event. Lastly, the effectiveness should consider the implications for outreach and evangelism: Were there Gospel-sharing opportunities among unbelievers? Were any directly converted/professed to be followers of faith? While these outcomes may be complex to quantify directly, it is essential to consider qualitative considerations.

Anecdotal evidence, testimonials, and follow-up conversations with attendees can provide valuable insights into the event's effectiveness in reaching the wider community. Collecting these testimonials through personal interviews or written submissions enables further understanding of the lived experiences of attendees and how the event impacted their beliefs and actions. Consider the event's alignment with the church's overall mission and vision. To what extent were the core values and beliefs of the church communicated through the event? Were the people it drew in aligned with the purpose and goals of the church? The demographics and background of the attendees will give insight into how well the event reached the targeted audience.

Measuring success in this aspect requires a clear understanding of the church's mission and the event's specific goals. By aligning event planning with the church's mission, the event's impact becomes more effectively measurable. Measuring the success of church events isn't a one-time activity. It's an ongoing process of reflection and evaluation. Review the data collected, analyze the results, and adjust your strategies accordingly. It's an iterative approach wherein one learns from the past, refines his method, and further improves his capability to build relationships and advance the Gospel message.

Be unafraid to try various approaches and techniques while always planning and assessing your work by seeking God's guidance and wisdom. Continual feedback from the attendees and church leadership will go a long way in refining future events and maximizing their impact. Arguably, the qualitative measurements of event success are the most important. While attendance gives a general measure of reach, the transformed life, strengthened faith, and deepened relationships brought forth by the event provide a more accurate measure of its success.

This holistic approach requires prayerful reflection, careful observation, and a readiness to adapt and refine strategies from gathered feedback. This holistic commitment to measurement helps ensure our church events are not simply an exercise in gathering but opportunities for authentic spiritual growth and the extension of God's Kingdom. Too often missed is the action that should be taken via feedback mechanisms. They should not be limited to after-the-event questionnaires; they should be included in every event segment. Consider including ways to obtain real-time feedback through quick comment cards or interactive polls during the event.

This enables one to make immediate changes and enhancements on the spot, keeping the event timely and relevant to the needs of the attendees. This also allows for immediate engagement with attendees, creating a more interactive and dynamic event experience. Furthermore, the long-term follow-up shouldn't be an afterthought; it's a crucial part of the process. Assign a team or individual to make follow-up calls with the attendees, provide resources, and foster continued involvement, thereby nurturing these relationships. In this way, what could have been just a temporary connection is fostered into long-term relationships within the church.

This will also help to reinforce the feeling of community and belonging that was started by the event. Ongoing follow-up communication, like newsletters or emails, helps remind people about the event and its message, calling them to more excellent reflection and involvement. Success in church events can only be multifaceted, involving quantitative and qualitative data in proper balance. It's not a head count, but heart changes, building the Body of Christ for eternity.

By adopting a holistic approach to spiritual growth, community engagement, outreach, and alignment with the church's mission, the actual impact can be measured, and the creation of meaningful experiences that glorify God and further His work on earth can be strived for. This holistic measurement shall be pursued in the continuous process of learning, adapting, and refining to make our events contribute toward the growth of the Kingdom in lasting and meaningful ways.

Chapter 8

Cultivating a Culture of Generosity

The Biblical Basis for Giving

Giving, primarily understood in terms of tithing or the giving of charitable contributions to the church, is rooted in the deepest cores of biblical teachings. More than a financial transaction, this profoundly spiritual matter reflects our relationship with God and understanding of His provision. The Bible consistently communicates that generosity, as a spiritual discipline, should not be carried out of obligation to meet a quota but rather as an overflow of gratitude and acknowledgment that God owns all things. Understanding this makes giving a non-burdensome task and a joyful expression of faith.

This understanding is rooted in a strong foundation built within the Old Testament. Tithing, the process of giving ten percent to the Lord, is evidenced through Leviticus, Deuteronomy, and especially Malachi. Tithing was not some legalistic principle to which the people had to adhere. Still, one specifically established to provide for the Levites who ministered in the Tabernacle and later in the temple to provide for the community as a whole. It was acknowledging God's sovereignty and participating in His work. Malachi 3:8-10 gives a powerful reminder of the blessings accompanying faithful giving: "Will a man rob God? Yet ye have robbed me. But ye say, wherein have we robbed thee? In tithes and offerings. Ye are cursed with a curse: for ye have robbed me, even this whole nation. Bring ye all the tithes into the storehouse, that there may be meat in mine house, and prove me now herewith, saith the Lord of hosts, if I will not open you the windows of heaven, and pour you out a blessing, that there shall not be room enough to receive it." This text emphasizes an essential principle in giving: this is not about depleting our resources but instead experiencing God's abundant provisions. It's an invitation to trust in God's faithfulness to supply our needs as we faithfully steward what He has entrusted us. The New Testament further expands on this theme, emphasizing the importance of giving materially and in terms of service and compassion. Jesus often spoke on generosity, teaching through parables like the Good Samaritan and the Widow's Mite on selfless giving and sacrificial love. The parable of the talents (Matthew 25:14-30) points out our responsibility to use our gifts and resources for God's glory. Those who were diligent with their talents were commended, while those who buried their talents were condemned for their lack of faithfulness. This parable is not only about money but about using every one of our abilities and resources, skills, influence, and finances to further God's kingdom.

The Apostle Paul, in his letters, also writes extensively on the issue of giving as he urged the churches he planted to share in the needs of other brethren. His instructions about the collections for the poor in Jerusalem in Romans 15:25-27, 1 Corinthians 16:1-4, and 2 Corinthians 8-9 show that sacrificial giving brings joy. Paul emphasizes the cheerful giving principle, which does not arise out of obligation but out of a heart bubbling with gratitude and love for God and other people. Second Corinthians 9:7 reinforces this: "Every man according as he purposed in his heart, so let him give; not grudgingly, or of necessity: for God loveth a cheerful giver." It is not enough for the attitude accompanying the giving to be pleasant. Instead, it conveys the spiritual principle that giving must come from a willing and cheerful spirit if it is to please God. Giving under pressure and because of guilt does not come from the heart.

The New Testament teaches that true wealth lies not in material possessions but in our relationship with God. Jesus' teachings on riches and poverty (Matthew 6:19-21; Luke 16:1-13) challenge us to consider our priorities and to avoid the pitfalls of accumulating wealth at the expense of our spiritual lives. The parable of the rich fool (Luke 12:16-21) serves as a cautionary tale, highlighting the futility of storing up treasures on earth while neglecting our eternal destiny. This doesn't advocate for poverty but encourages us to view our resources through a spiritual lens, recognizing that everything we possess is a gift from God to be used for His glory and the benefit of others.

But, as one can learn, generosity in the Bible doesn't start and stop with just dollars-and-cents giving. God has entrusted us with talents, resources, relationships, and time, which involve a greater understanding of stewardship. According to this view, each person is called to exercise faithfulness in their stewardship by being purposeful in using one's gifts and resources to touch other people's lives for the glory of God. It involves conscious choices about how we spend our time, use our skills, and manage our finances. It's a holistic approach to living a life pleasing to God, where generosity permeates every aspect of our existence.

This understanding of biblical generosity should shape how churches approach financial giving. While it is necessary, financial giving is not all about collecting money for a church's operational needs. It's about creating a generous culture where members feel they can give joyfully and sacrificially, knowing that God is using their resources for more excellent work. This means adopting transparent and accountable financial practices: keeping the church's money "to be used appropriately" and effectively to achieve what God is trying to accomplish.

Second, churches should make it a point to teach and model generosity intentionally, communicating both the spiritual benefits of living generously and how much living advances God's kingdom. This would include testifying how God has used the church's generosity to impact lives within the congregation and the community. It also allows the members to participate in different forms of giving other than just writing checks, such as volunteering time, sharing skills, and other acts of service.

The biblical basis for giving is not a set of rigid rules but a foundational principle rooted in gratitude, faith, and love. It's the call to participate in God's work, use our resources for His glory, and experience the joy and blessings accompanying a life of generosity. It's a holistic approach to life that changes our relationship with God and the world around us. Understanding this deep spiritual dimension of giving equips the church to create a culture of generosity in which people are generous financially and further God's kingdom in every aspect of life. It takes the understanding of giving from being transactional to transformational in faith and grace, as expected from a loving and generous God.

Communicating the Vision of Generosity

Communicating a vision of generosity isn't just about asking for money; it's painting a compelling picture of how sacrificial giving fuels the church's mission and changes lives.

This requires a movement beyond the transactional requests to a heartfelt commitment to partner with God in His work in the kingdom. To this end, effective ministry leaders need a strategic, heartfelt communication plan that reaches the hearts of their congregants.

First, the vision must be clearly defined. What specific goals does the church want to reach through member generosity? Is it investing in local missions, international outreach, building renovation, or youth programs? The vision statement needs to articulate these goals concisely and clearly while underlining the impact of giving to make a difference in people's lives and furthering God's kingdom. Avoid generalities, concretize examples, and illustrate with compelling stories. For example, instead of saying, "We need to raise funds for our building project," say, "Through your generosity, we can create a welcoming space that will foster deeper spiritual growth and provide a haven for our community, creating opportunities for hundreds to encounter Christ." The financial request has become a story of hope and transformation.

Once defined, that vision needs to be communicated. This will be accomplished by using various streams to speak to all congregants. The website shall have a dedicated page that describes the vision, enumerates the different ways of giving, and shows the result of past contributions through testimonials, photos, and videos. The church bulletin shall regularly update the progress of ministry initiatives funded by generous giving in stories of changed lives. Regular announcements during services should request donations and share inspiring stories of the work being accomplished thanks to the congregation's generosity.

Also, consider posting to social media platforms to share updates and encourage giving. Short, engaging videos can be a powerful testament to the difference donations are making. Keep in mind that social media is a visual medium; impactful visuals are what will speak volumes. Consider before-and-after photos of a renovation project or share testimonials of those whose lives have been impacted by the church's ministries. This should be an emotional way to connect with the congregation, proving how their contributions make a tangible difference.

Beyond digital platforms, organize events to showcase the church's vision of generosity. A unique service dedicated to giving might include missionary testimonies, recipients of church programs, or even leaders who oversee the disbursement of funds. This is a powerful opportunity to connect the dots between giving and real-world impact. Also, open houses or tours of improved or constructed facilities made possible by the collective generosity of the church could be effective. Sometimes, visual demonstrations of the fruit that comes through giving can affect a deep and broad understanding of their contribution among congregation members.

Be transparent. Communicate regularly how gifts are utilized through detailed financial reports and updates regarding the ministry's initiatives. This accountability builds trust and encourages people to continue being generous. Consider developing a system to track contributions and their outcomes, making the data available to the congregation through easily digestible reports. It shows that the church is committed to responsible stewardship.

Again, encourage a culture of gratitude: let the congregation know, with regular thanks, just how much their largesse is appreciated. This could come as personal thank-you notes, emails, or phone calls that mean so much. The action may be practical by being made public during services or within the church bulletin. Gratitude fosters generosity.

Training is key. The members must be equipped with knowledge and skills to communicate the church's vision of generosity effectively. Training on how to speak to others about giving, answering tricky questions, and sharing compelling stories will better equip them to be ambassadors for the church's vision, which multiplies the impact of your communication efforts. Also, consider workshops or seminars focusing on biblical stewardship, emphasizing the spiritual nature of giving.

Use storytelling in this communication strategy. Share uplifting stories of how God has used the generosity of the church to impact people's lives, not only inside the congregation but also beyond. These stories can have a strong emotional appeal to the audience and may be more memorable and convincing. Use real participants who can convey their experiences. This kind of presentation adds to their credibility and can create deeper connections.

Beyond individual stories, consider highlighting the broader impact of collective giving. Show how the congregation's combined generosity has accomplished great things, exceeded expectations, and made a significant difference in the lives of many. This collaborative approach can inspire individuals to participate more fully, realizing their contribution as part of a more extensive, transformative work.

Consider using different communication styles to appeal to the variety of personalities in your congregation. While logical arguments and data may touch some more, others might need a bit of emotion in the argument and some inspiration via stories. A multidimensional approach, employing multiple tools and styles, will go a long way in creating an inclusive and effective strategy. This involves using different visual media, such as images, videos, and infographics, since people have different learning styles.

Besides formal channels, they provide an avenue for informal conversation regarding generosity. Engage in the training of the leadership and members to help organically incorporate the concept at an organic level of one-on-one discussions through real life. This approach has helped establish a culture of openly sharing and celebrating giving. This, too, can make the connection way more personal and make the environment much warmer when considering generosity.

Building a generous culture requires persistence rather than being an overnight happening. Communication needs to be consistent. The church's vision should be regularly reinforced, along with updates on ministry initiatives, and appreciation should be communicated for the congregation's contribution. Consistently communicating the vision of generosity allows the church to create a deep commitment to faithful, sacrificial giving, which enables the congregation to partner with God in changing lives and advancing His kingdom. This is not just asking for money; it is about provoking hearts to be involved in God's work and recognizing the transformative power of generosity.

Developing Giving Strategies That Align with Values

Building giving programs in a way that aligns with the values of a church requires a very thoughtful and strategic approach. It is not about coming up with mechanisms for collecting funds but about building opportunities for actual participation in God's work, reflecting the core beliefs and mission of the church. This involves understanding spiritual maturity, capacity for giving, and overall understanding of stewardship within the congregation. A successful giving program equips people to give joyfully, sacrificially, and purposefully, knowing that their gifts are deeply connected to actual results in the lives of others.

Clearly define the mission and values of the church. What is the core purpose behind your ministry? Do you focus on local outreach, international missions, youth programs, or a combination of ministries? By articulating these specific goals, the church gets a framework to design confident giving programs to facilitate these initiatives directly. For example, a church that supports global missions can establish one giving fund to support missionaries, while a church emphasizing community development may establish one to support local outreach programs. With this clarity, every given contribution has a tangible, visible purpose to which all may connect more meaningfully and participate. Transparency is key here: communicating where the money goes and how donations make a difference builds trust and promotes further generosity.

Consider the methods of giving. Besides the traditional offering plate, explore other options to appeal to different preferences and comfort levels with technology. Online giving platforms, text-to-give options, and recurring giving programs offer flexibility and convenience. Web-based giving solutions integrate with many churches' accounting systems, making it an easy and seamless process while updating the giving in real time. Text-to-give allows for quick and easy donations, particularly appealing to younger generations accustomed to mobile transactions. Recurring giving programs, in which donors commit to giving regularly, offer predictable income streams, enabling better financial planning for the church. The key is to provide multiple channels, ensuring accessibility for everyone within the congregation.

When designing your giving programs, remember to address different giving capacities. Not all members have the same financial resources. Creating various giving opportunities, from small, recurring donations to larger, one-time gifts, accommodates varying levels of financial commitment. This inclusive approach ensures that every member can participate meaningfully, regardless of their financial situation. Consider calling out the impact of smaller gifts, touting how many gifts come together to make more significant impacts possible. This could be shared in stories about how smaller donations exceptionally impacted specific ministry initiatives.

In addition to financial support, consider soliciting opportunities for non-monetary types of giving. Most people have unique skills or talents that would be valuable to the church. Programs utilizing such resources will help build and instill a sense of belonging and shared responsibility among members. This may take the form of volunteering with church activities, providing pro bono professional services within the realms of accounting, marketing, or construction, or sharing creative talents to empower worship. By acknowledging the value of these contributions, the church can build an even wealthier culture of giving beyond what's in one's wallet.

Teach biblical principles of stewardship to the congregation. This is not just about asking for money but about developing a deeper understanding of how God entrusts resources to each individual and how responsible management of those resources reflects a commitment to His kingdom. Regular teaching on biblical stewardship, replete with relevant scriptures and practical examples, can transform the perspective on giving. This education must emphasize the joy and blessing of giving rather than being a burden or obligation. Sharing personal testimonies of how giving has blessed individuals can be powerful in touching others to adopt a generous spirit.

Make gratitude a core part of your giving programs. Expressing genuine appreciation for every contribution, regardless of size, is essential. This may be accomplished through verbal recognitions at services, personalized notes of thanks, and/or regular updates in church newsletters regarding the impact of giving. A simple "thank you" can be done, as that makes them feel so good and appreciated. Publicly recognizing significant donations or a long-term commitment to giving can inspire others. However, let recognition be done sensitively and respectfully without putting pressure or comparing givers.

Create transparency and accountability in the culture. Keep communicating the usage of donations. Give detailed financial reports on income and expenses, highlighting the positive impacts of contributions to different ministry initiatives. These build trust and reinforce the idea that donations are managed responsibly and effectively. Consider organizing events that showcase the results of the church's outreach programs, demonstrating how contributions are making a real difference in the lives of others. This transparency ensures donors feel confident that their contributions are making a tangible and positive impact.

Incorporate storytelling into your giving strategies. Nothing touches the congregation's hearts like compelling stories of how church ministries have changed people's lives. The stories show how, through giving, the church can reach out to the community, care for the needy, and advance the Kingdom of God. These should be genuine and personal stories, not clichéd or sentimental. They should illustrate the power of transformation both receiving and giving will have. The culture of generosity needs to be long-term in nature. That is to say, constant effort, thoughtful planning, and a genuine desire to raise a giving spirit in the congregation. Regularly reevaluate your giving programs and make changes based on responses and observations. Be prepared to adjust your strategies accordingly to fit your congregation's changing needs and preferences. Always remind the congregation of the church's vision, values, and mission, in which generosity plays an essential role in achieving the church's goals. Through these ways, you can create giving programs that would provide for the church's financial needs and establish a deep culture of generosity in the congregation, transforming hearts and aligning their giving with their faith and God's kingdom work. This holistic approach ensures that giving becomes a joyful act of worship, strengthening the bonds within the church community and enabling it to fulfill its mission effectively.

Educating Members on Stewardship

Stewardship education with our members is more than teaching them how to write a check or swipe a debit card. It is about fostering a deep understanding of their relationship with God and the place their resources play within that relationship. This begins with a biblical foundation for the teaching, using scripture, and applying it to everyday life. We need to get beyond the declaration that God owns all and show how that reality touches every aspect of life in our decisions about money, time, and talents.

One practical approach is to use biblical narratives to illustrate the principles of stewardship. For example, the story of the talents in Matthew 25 is not just a parable on investing money. Still, it's a strong and powerful example of how God entrusts us with resources, time, abilities, and finances and expects us to use them responsibly and productively in His kingdom. We could take this story as an opportunity to discuss using our talents and resources to advance God's work. We can encourage members to identify their "talents" and brainstorm how to utilize those gifts to benefit the church and the wider community.

Another powerful tool is to explore the concept of abundance versus scarcity. Many people approach finances from a place of scarcity, believing they have limited resources and must hoard what they have. The Bible, however, teaches us about God's abundant provision. Deuteronomy 8:18 promises that God gives us the power to get wealth. This verse doesn't promise wealth to everyone, but it highlights the principle that our ability to acquire resources comes from God. Teaching our members about God's abundance encourages them to view their resources not as a source of anxiety but as a blessing to be shared. Discussions can focus on how looking at their finances through God's abundance can change their perspective and lead to greater giving.

We need to talk about debt. Many people are in debt, significantly affecting their ability to give freely. Addressing debt directly in our teaching may be necessary. We can provide resources and workshops on financial literacy and debt management. It must be presented instead as a supportive program that enables all members to surmount some financial obstacles and taste the freedom of responsible economic management. We can collaborate with reputable financial advisors or even use online resources to deliver practical ways of reducing debt and living within one's budget. They hope to assume responsibility for their lives, leading them to a more relaxed and generous spirit.

Beyond finances, we have to highlight stewardship of time and talent. While many members may be eager to serve, they often struggle to carve out time to commit to a particular ministry. We can provide some practical ways of managing time and challenge the members to identify areas where they can serve effectively without getting overwhelmed. This could mean providing flexible volunteer opportunities or encouraging the delegation of responsibilities. We can also engage members in discovering and using their spiritual gifts. We will have access to assessments and discussion groups, which will enlighten their strengths and ways in which they can apply their strength to benefit the church and community.

Transparency plays a significant role in training the members on stewardship. For instance, it is considered vital to open the budget and financial reports of the church. This encourages transparency and accountability. People give much more generously when they understand how their contributions are used. We can help people understand the church's financial statements in plain, easy-to-understand language, pointing out the impact of their giving. We can also highlight specific projects and ministries that have been made possible through the donations of members, showing them the actual outcomes of their generosity.

We can provide opportunities for our members to discuss stewardship meaningfully. Small group studies, workshops, or even casual conversations can help members gain greater insight and cultivate a sense of generosity. Inspirational case studies of people blessed through faithful stewardship may also be used. Sharing stories of God's provision for the church and individuals through members' faithful giving is an assertive means of reinforcing the principles of stewardship.

We must resource our people to make informed decisions: how-to guides, online portals, and regular communications about the church's financial needs. In this way, giving becomes easier and more accessible. We can also promote giving through various methods, such as online giving, text-to-give, or traditional offerings, to accommodate different preferences. The goal is not to compel members to give but to make the process easy and smooth.

Besides teaching, we need to emphasize the joy of giving. Giving is not a burden; it is a privilege. Acts of generosity bring spiritual fulfillment and a deeper connection with God. We can share testimonials from members who have experienced the joy of giving and its positive impact on their lives. We can encourage a culture of gratitude, reminding members to thank God for their blessings and to express appreciation for the opportunities they have to give.

We need to nurture a culture of generosity continuously. Stewardship education is not something that happens once; it's ongoing. We must regularly reinforce stewardship principles through sermons, small group discussions, and church-wide initiatives. It, therefore, remains upon us how to bake these principles into our Church culture, the DNA through which generosity may become so natural a part of our lives. As this is true of stewardship, putting it in several parts throughout the church and giving within our community touches every point. Through this holistic approach, giving becomes more than a financial transaction; it is a spiritual practice that enhances the lives of our members and further equips our community to fulfill its mission. This will change the hearts of our members as they adopt generosity as a lifestyle, an expression of God's love, and a reflection of their faith.

Building Trust and Transparency in Finances

Building trust in a church's financial management is paramount. It's not just a question of legality but of fostering deep confidence and faith in the members. When members feel their contributions are handled responsibly and ethically, their generosity flows more freely, and their spiritual connection to the church deepens. Transparency, therefore, is not only a best practice but a spiritual mandate.

Clear and consistent communication is one of the best ways to engender this trust. This is more than publishing an annual budget; it is periodic reporting about the church's financial status. Consider setting up a section on the church's website that outlines income and expenses. This may include monthly or quarterly reports showing where donations go to ministry programs, building maintenance, salaries of staff members, and outreach. Transparency lets the members see the tangible way their money serves and involves them personally in the church's mission. This information should be given in an easily understandable format without using all the technical accounting terms. Use charts, graphs, and simple summaries to make the financial information accessible to everyone, regardless of financial literacy.

Regular communication doesn't stop at the website. Include updates in the church bulletin, during service announcements, or even through a dedicated newsletter. Consider organizing an annual financial forum where church leaders can openly address questions and concerns about the church's finances. This would allow for a direct interaction where members can have a dialogue and better understand the financial stewardship of the church. The forum should present the numbers and explain the 'whys' of the economic decisions, emphasizing the strategic goals of the church and how the financial resources contribute to achieving those goals.

Beyond presenting the numbers, it is essential to show the processes through which financial decisions are made. Establishing a clear economic policy approved by the church's governing body will instill confidence. This policy should outline the roles and responsibilities of those handling church finances, including budgeting, spending, and auditing procedures. Making this policy readily available to the congregation demonstrates a commitment to accountability and good governance. The policy should also detail conflict of interest protocols and procedures for handling potential irregularities. This proactive approach shows the church's commitment to ethical practices and instills confidence in its members, who might raise one or two concerns.

Independent audits are very crucial for building trust. Hiring the services of a reputable independent accounting firm to audit regularly offers third-party verification of the church's financial practices. The audit report should be available to the congregation, and it will not only highlight the economic health of the church but also confirm that the church's financial records are accurate and reliable. This external validation reinforces the church's commitment to transparency and accountability, reassuring members that their donations are managed with integrity. This also helps to safeguard the church from potential misunderstandings and allegations of misappropriation of funds.

In addition to formal audits, consider using sound internal controls. This includes separating duties, requiring multiple signatures on significant transactions, and maintaining detailed records of all financial activities. A sound internal control system helps prevent errors and fraud and sends a positive message to the congregation regarding responsible economic management. Regular training of those responsible for the church's finances will ensure they know the latest techniques and comply with all related regulations. This will also help in easy knowledge and responsibility transfer in case there is any change in personnel.

Beyond the formal mechanisms of transparency, a culture of openness has to be promoted. Encourage open dialogue about financial matters within the church community. Allow a safe place for questions and concerns, where members can feel comfortable airing their inquiries without fear of judgment. This can be accommodated in small group discussions, pastoral counseling, or dedicated Q&A sessions during church services. Active listening and respectful responses are essential in building trust and creating a culture of openness.

Building trust is a process, not an event. Consistency in communication, transparency in actions, and a proactive approach to concerns will go a long way in maintaining this vital relationship with the membership. Regularly review and update financial policies and procedures to reflect best practices and adapt to changing circumstances. In demonstrating a commitment to financial integrity, churches build trust and cultivate a thriving culture of generosity.

Adding an option to your church website devoted to financial FAQs. Consider forewarning questions regarding the fate of donations, church budget management, and some financial accountability. Easy-to-access information equips church members with an understanding that will help them have peace of mind without fears of anxiety or apprehension over uncertainties within your church. Make updates whenever changes to your church finances or any process change. Provide contact details of church personnel whom parishioners can consult for more information.

Engage active church members in financial matters. This may include creating a finance committee of the church volunteers from the congregation. This committee can give oversight, contribute to the decision-making of budgetary questions, and review financial reports. The engagement of members ensures necessary input and builds a sense of shared responsibility and ownership of the church's economic welfare. Selection to the Finance Committee should be made transparently, considering membership that reflects diversity in experience and expertise. Similarly, the induction of committee members through periodic training will lead to members being well-equipped to perform assigned duties.

Consider the diversity in background and financial literacy within your congregation. Avoid using jargon or complicated terms when communicating financial information. Use simple language and visual aids to ensure everyone understands the church's economic situation. This is considerate of all members and helps to build trust by making sure everyone is informed and involved. Offer multiple ways to access financial information, catering to different communication preferences. Offer written reports and audio/video presentations.

Building trust involves integrity with the numbers and everyday aspects of the church's life. As members see honesty and transparency regarding other areas of church operations, they will begin to trust how it manages its finances. Continual ethical behavior brings on board credibility and a closer community with one's faith. This includes transparency in leadership decisions, open communication regarding church events and activities, and ethical conduct within all church ministries. A church that demonstrates integrity speaks volumes about trustworthiness, enhancing the community's bond of faith and generosity.

Chapter 9

Measuring Success Beyond Numbers

Defining Spiritual Growth Metrics

The traditional metrics of business website traffic, social media engagement, and attendance numbers far too often fall short as metrics for church outreach. While these numbers can sometimes provide a glimpse into the activity level, they do not capture the essence of spiritual growth, the change in lives, or any strengthening of faith communities. To understand the effectiveness of a church's marketing efforts, we need to move beyond the superficial and focus on the qualitative aspects of spiritual impact. This requires defining and tracking metrics individually and collectively that reflect true transformation.

Defining meaningful spiritual growth metrics requires a shift in perspective. We move away from a purely quantitative approach, focusing instead on the qualitative changes occurring within individuals and the community. Instead of counting heads, we assess the depth of faith, the transformation of hearts, and the demonstrable impact on lives. This requires a more subtle understanding of what constitutes genuine spiritual growth within the church's mission and vision.

One key metric would be personal spiritual maturity. It is less quantitative than qualitative and can only be observed in changed lives, deepening faith, and increased spiritual disciplines. Are people attending Bible studies, prayer, or small groups? Are they serving others inside and outside the church with increased devotion? Are people in personal discipleship or seeking spiritual formation? These qualitative measures provide a much richer picture than mere attendance counts. Consider developing a simple observation rubric or survey to capture anecdotal data in these areas. For instance, questions such as "How has your faith deepened in the past year?" or "In what ways are you serving others?" may prove enlightening.

Another key area to explore is life transformation. Are people being healed in various ways, such as emotionally or spiritually? Are lives affected by the Gospel's power, giving them meaning and direction? Are improvements witnessed in attitudes, conduct, and relationships due to personal dependence on God? Collect testimony or interview members for possible outcomes of such change. These stories help demonstrate the impact of the church's ministry and further inspire others on their journey of faith. These stories are not just anecdotes but strong data points depicting the qualitative success of your outreach.

Beyond individual transformation, we have to look at the health and growth of the community as well. A healthy community will have good relationships, people looking out for each other, and a sense of purpose. Are members actively involved in fellowship and community events? Is there a spirit of unity and mutual encouragement amongst the congregation? Do the members feel they belong and are supported? It is essential to take regular surveys, focus groups, and even casual observations to get insight into all these areas regarding community health. The frequency of acts of service amongst the congregation and their involvement in outreach initiatives can also be measured for valuable data.

Another critical metric is the effectiveness of discipleship programs. Are people in mentoring relationships? Are they growing in their understanding and application of biblical principles? Are they equipped to share their faith with others? The progress of individuals within the discipleship programs and the assessment of spiritual growth provides valuable insights into the effectiveness of these formative initiatives. This may include tracking attendance, assignment participation, and personal reflections. Regular contact with mentors and mentees is vital to understanding the quality of these relationships and resulting spiritual growth.

Equally important is gauging the effectiveness of the church's outreach into the greater community. Is there observable positive change within the community due to the church's ministry? Are relationships being developed with local organizations and community leaders? Is the church effectively addressing local needs and providing tangible support? This might involve tracking the number of community events the church participates in, the number of people served through outreach programs, and feedback from community partners. Consider partnering with community organizations to quantify the impact of your combined efforts.

Evaluating these qualitative metrics requires a structured approach. Developing a clear framework for data collection, analysis, and interpretation is crucial. These may include the following: surveys, interviews, focus groups, observation checklists, and testimonials. Data collected will be analyzed qualitatively for patterns, trends, and insights, rather than numerical outcomes. Any attempt at evaluation must be undertaken in a spirit of humility, recognizing that God's ways are not our ways and the fruits of ministry are often long-term. The importance of celebration and reflection. Regularly reviewing the collected data, celebrating successes, and learning from challenges with determination are vital for continuous improvement. This process helps refine outreach strategies, ensures efforts remain aligned with the church's mission, and fosters a culture of ongoing growth and development. These reflections shouldn't just be a yearly exercise but an ongoing dialogue within the church leadership and amongst the congregation. Sharing successes and challenges openly builds trust and encourages a culture of learning and mutual support. This continuous feedback loop is critical for refining the church's approach to outreach and maximizing its long-term impact. By shifting from a numbers focus to a qualitative assessment of spiritual impact, churches are better able to understand how effective they are in service to the communities they wish to reach. This holistic approach allows a deeper understanding of God's work and provides a framework for genuine, sustainable, and impactful ministry.

Assessing the Transformation of Lives

It requires a shift in our thinking to measure life transformation; simple metrics will not get it. Website hits and Facebook 'likes' give a picture of the activity level, but they do not tell how spiritual growth is taking place in people's lives. To accurately assess the effectiveness of our church outreach, we need to design some type of system for tracking the qualitative impact of our ministry. It means grasping the multifaceted ways God is at work in people's lives and developing ways to measure that change. This will make us closer to being spiritually aware.

One tangible way to do this comes from personal testimonies. Ask your congregation to share their stories of how God has used the ministries of your church-the sermon, small group, community outreach event, or online resource-to bring about such changes in them. These testimonies are not anecdotal but are concrete realities that testify to the change of heart. By collecting these narratives and then analyzing them, one can outline common themes, patterns of spiritual growth, and point of greatest impact by our ministries. These stories are powerful for assessment and inspire and encourage the congregation and the church leadership. We need to provide a conducive environment where people can share their vulnerabilities and celebrate their victories. Consider setting up a section on the church website or a time in the services for testimony sharing. This can be complemented with personal, one-on-one discussions to gain a deeper understanding of the person's spiritual journey.

Apart from personal testimony, we can also assess transformation by observing behavior and lifestyle changes. Has anyone overcome a particular struggle or addiction through the care and discipleship provided by the church? Are there noticeable changes in their prayer life, Bible study, or service to others? Are they engaging in discipleship relationships, mentoring others, or demonstrating more significant commitment to living out their faith in daily life? These changes in behavior are quite tangible in terms of spiritual development and therefore should be viewed as important measures of success. We may want to explore using anonymized surveys or feedback forms related to key behaviors and spiritual disciplines along with community engagement as part of tracking such areas. Such questionnaires should refrain from being intrusive or judgmental and be aimed toward growth and positive changes.

The results need to inform and shape future ministry initiatives so that our understanding is refined regarding what truly works.

Measuring life transformation needs to include ways to determine if our faith communities are growing and healthy. Are the small groups healthy? Are people supporting and encouraging one another? Is there a sense of belonging/fellowship within the congregation? These reflect a healthy spiritual environment and an effective outreach. We must move beyond counting the number of people attending services and delve into the quality of relationships and the depth of spiritual connection within those groups. This could involve conducting group evaluations or facilitating focus groups to gain feedback on the effectiveness of small groups and other community-building initiatives. Are individuals feeling supported, challenged, and spiritually nourished within the church community? Open communication and feedback mechanisms are critical for understanding the needs and experiences of our congregants.

Another key element is evaluating the church's impact on the broader community. Has our outreach program led to increased involvement in local charities or social justice initiatives? Are we seeing positive changes in our relationships with neighboring organizations or community leaders? Is our presence a blessing to the community around us, reflecting the love and grace of Christ? A successful church outreach program is one that is not limited to the confines of the church itself but spreads its influence to the greater community. Measuring the impact to the community must involve careful deliberation on the goals and purposes of our community outreach. Are we trying to fill some particular need in the community? Are we developing partnerships with local organizations to solve social problems? Are we working at being a source of hope and change in our community? Effectiveness will need to include ways to measure the outcomes of our efforts in the greater community-surveying partnering organizations, for example, or polling the community.

The process of assessing transformation requires careful planning and implementation. We need to come up with SMART goals that are in agreement with the mission and vision of our church. These goals should focus on numerical growth and qualitative spiritual and community development aspects. That is, to clearly state indicators of transformation which can be monitored and measured through time. Example: A SMART goal could be, "Increase the number of congregants actively participating in at least one small group by 25% in the next six months." Or "Increase the number of community service projects participated in by members by 15% over the next year." These goals should be reviewed regularly and adjusted according to the changing needs of the congregation and community.

Remember, it is ongoing assessment and refinement. Continually collect data, analyze results, and use what was learned to adapt strategies accordingly. This should be a collaborative process among the church leadership, ministry leaders, and congregation members. It involves a culture of transparency and accountability within the church. This will build ownership and a sense of community, helping us all to identify areas where we need to work together to improve. Regularly scheduled reviews, incorporating feedback from several sources, will help ensure our outreach efforts are indeed effective and within the will of God.

The place of prayer and discernment: While providing relative success in life transformations, we should always be willing to seek God's guidance and wisdom. We must lean upon the Holy Spirit to show us where our ministries are touching and leading others. Our evaluations should not be strictly based on measurable results but on prayerful reflection and discerning the movement of the Holy Spirit within the church and the community. In all this, regular prayer and seeking God's guidance become imperative.

Successes must be celebrated. We must acknowledge and celebrate God's work when we see evidence of transformation in individuals and communities. This not only builds morale and encourages further efforts but also strengthens the faith and commitment of the congregation. Celebrating success can involve recognizing individuals who have shown significant growth, highlighting the positive impact of specific ministries, or simply sharing testimonies of God's faithfulness. These can be the kind of celebrations that facilitate a spirit of gratitude and reinforce positive ministry efforts that inspire growth and transformation.

By adding the qualitative means of assessment to the prayerful approach, a far better holistic understanding of the impact our church's outreach is making can be achieved. This leads to authentic and sustainable growth within the church and the larger community for a more dynamic, faithful expression of God's kingdom. The ultimate measure of success is not just numbers but rather the evidence of transformed lives, faith strengthened, and communities transformed by the love of Christ.

Monitoring Community Engagement and Relationships

The basis of all good church outreach is a real relationship. While the numbers indicate something of the activity of the ministry, they cannot capture what a real relationship and community growth are all about. The ability to track community engagement in relationships requires a paradigm shift: from a strictly quantitative monitoring to a more holistic qualitative one. It involves actively listening to the needs of our community, fostering a sense of belonging, and nurturing relationships based on mutual respect and genuine care. It's about recognizing that each individual is a unique creation of God, deserving of personalized attention and support.

One effective strategy is through regular touchpoints with the congregants and community members. It will also involve weekly or monthly newsletters that are not necessarily an announcement but include personal stories, reflections, and opportunities for connections. Think of including a "Member Spotlight" section in your newsletter-a segment showcasing the different talents and contributions of individuals and families making up your congregation, along with their testimonies. This engenders community and a stronger sense of bonding among people. Beyond the newsletters, organizing periodic social gatherings and fellowship events provides invaluable opportunities for informal interaction and relationship building. These can be anything from casual coffee mornings to themed dinners, family picnics, or even volunteer projects within the community. The key is to create spaces where people feel comfortable interacting, sharing, and connecting on a deeper level.

We need to put in place mechanisms for monitoring contact other than just attendance. This could be as simple as a feedback mechanism through comment cards or online surveys of input regarding services, events, and general satisfaction.

These mechanisms are not to be used just to solve complaints and discover ways in which we can better serve and connect with the community, but the information derived from them should be proactively used to refine the programs and events to better meet the needs of those involved. It involves active listening-not just hearing but attempting to understand the underlying concerns, feelings, and experiences of people in our church and community.

Other than formal surveys, informal meetings are also very relevant. Pastors, church leaders, and volunteers need to have one-on-one personal interactions with congregants. Little things, like remembering birthdays, giving a listening ear, or making an effort to understand the problems of each individual, help build trust and deeper relationships. This also involves a concerted effort to reach out to new members and visitors, warmly welcoming them and helping them integrate into the church community. Remember, incorporating new members takes time and consistent effort. It involves introducing them to other members, inviting them to small groups or ministry teams, and generally creating opportunities for them to feel accepted and included. This approach extends beyond the church walls to encompass the wider community.

The church should be actively involved in community events and partnerships. This could be through volunteering at local charities, sponsoring community events, or organizing interfaith events that show a commitment to serving beyond the church walls. Building relationships with leaders of other regional organizations, such as schools, community centers, and businesses, provides opportunities for cross-promotion and collaboration on shared community goals. These partnerships can increase visibility, improve community relations, and a broader reach for the church's message.

However, monitoring relationships also involves sensitivity to individuals' emotional and spiritual well-being. It is crucial to identify members who may be struggling or facing challenges. This requires being attentive to subtle cues, such as changes in behavior, reduced participation, or expressions of distress. The church should have systems to offer support and assistance, connecting individuals with appropriate resources, pastoral care, or counseling services as needed. The aim is to increase attendance and make it a caring, loving environment where people are looked after and taken care of.

Technology plays an important role in improving communication and building relationships. While social media can be an effective medium, one must know how to use it judiciously and with authenticity. Your focus should be on creating engaging content that fosters connection and encourages interaction. This might mean posting upbeat stories, behind-the-scenes insights into the church, or even calls for people to interact online. Just don't let yourself become obsessed with finding those likes and followers. It is not about going viral but interacting and creating relationships. In the same light, keep in mind how limited life on social media can be. It does not need to replace direct contact with real-life interaction.

Church management software tracks member information, volunteer involvement, and event participation. This data helps identify patterns, understand member needs, and personalize outreach efforts. It can also help in communication with members through email, text messaging, or other digital platforms, creating a more streamlined and efficient system for communication. This digital strategy should supplement, not replace, personal interaction. The goal remains to build genuine relationships and provide personalized care.

Another crucial aspect of relationship building is effective conflict resolution. Disagreements and conflicts are inevitable within any community, including a church. A transparent process for addressing concerns and resolving disputes peacefully and biblically is crucial for maintaining a healthy and harmonious environment. This involves training church leaders and members on effective conflict-resolution strategies, establishing clear communication channels, and fostering a culture of empathy and forgiveness.

We need to constantly evaluate and adapt our strategies. Periodically assessing the effectiveness of outreach, soliciting feedback from members and the community, and adjusting based on the data collected will ensure we are always refining our approach. This might include periodic surveys, focus groups, or one-on-one interviews to gain insight into the perceptions and needs of the community. Remember that growth isn't linear, and continuous adjustment must remain relevant and effective in a dynamic context. The ultimate goal is to create a vibrant, welcoming, and loving community where people experience God's transformative love and grace.

Monitoring community engagement and relationships requires a multifaceted approach beyond numerical metrics. It means listening actively to the needs of our community, fostering a sense of belonging, and nurturing relationships based on mutual respect, genuine care, and deep commitment to serving others with God's love. Embracing qualitative and quantitative assessments, using appropriate technological tools wisely, and continuing to adapt our strategies will make for a more vibrant and effective church community that reflects the transformative power of Christ in our world. Success is not measured by the numbers we round up, but in the lives that are touched, the relationships strengthened, and communities transformed by the grace and love of God.

Evaluating Discipleship and Spiritual Formation

Evaluation of the success of our church's outreach is not about merely counting heads or website clicks. Real growth, as the previous chapter made clear, is about people's spiritual flourishing and the strengthening of our community. This requires us to move away from a purely numerical focus toward a more holistic evaluation of our discipleship and spiritual formation initiatives. How might we measure the impact of our efforts beyond mere attendance figures? How do we measure the authentic spiritual development of the people involved in our programs?

One important aspect is the intentional design of discipleship programs themselves. Are our programs designed in a way that will effectively bring about spiritual change in people's lives? Do our programs include time for intentional spiritual practices in prayer, Bible study, and reflection? A well-structured program would lead people sequentially toward better understanding God's Word, better relational intimacy with Christ, and better abilities to live the Christian life. This must not be presumed; it needs to be tracked and measured.

Consider embedding regular check-ins and feedback mechanisms within your discipleship programs. These should not be formal, rigid assessments but opportunities for open conversation and mutual encouragement. A simple question,

"How has your understanding of God's love deepened in the last few weeks?" can reveal far more than a numerical attendance assessment. These conversations can be facilitated in small groups, allowing for a more personal and supportive environment. The goal isn't to judge but to provide pastoral care and support, allowing a more accurate assessment of individual spiritual growth.

Incorporating qualitative data collection is essential. This moves beyond simple quantitative measures like attendance numbers. Consider using surveys, questionnaires, or informal interviews to gauge participants' spiritual growth. Ask open-ended questions that encourage honest reflection on their faith journey. For example, "How has your relationship with God changed since you joined this program?" or "How has your understanding of the Bible deepened through your participation?" The responses to these questions offer invaluable insights into the effectiveness of your discipleship program, far exceeding what mere attendance figures can tell us.

Observational data can also play an important role in spiritual formation evaluation. Are participants showing an increasing devotion to prayer and Bible study? Are they becoming more compassionate and empathetic towards others? Do they actively pursue opportunities for service within the church and community? These behaviors are often more telling about spiritual growth than self-reported feelings. Those in the mentor and leader roles within the discipleship program are especially poised to observe these behavioral changes, thus offering another layer of qualitative assessment.

Remember that spiritual growth is nonlinear-it goes up and down. Sometimes people do not move for a long time, and even at times they regress. The implication, then, is that any attempt to measure spiritual formation has to be patient and understanding and long-term. Holistic assessment takes into account peaks and valleys; indeed, most actual growth is marked by the capacity to bounce back or survive hard times. It will not be a one-time assessment but must be done regularly to accurately determine whether the discipleship program is successful and effective.

The other key aspect of evaluation is the measurement that must be done beyond what is happening within the context of the program. The question is, does he manifest his faith in everyday living, at work, in the school, and in his home? This is the most overlooked measure. It is not an intellectual understanding that is required from the process of discipleship but transformational action. We would have to look at how well they incorporate faith into everyday living. This could be a no-agenda conversation, a follow-up session, or even asking feedback from the immediate family members or closest friends for an outside observation of the person's change.

The process of evaluation should not stop at the level of individual growth in discipleship but also in making the church community stronger. Do the discipleship programs in your church help people build and develop relationships? Do the programs provide a place of acceptance, value, and empowerment to share faith? A healthy community is accepting, supportive, encouraging, and committed to living out its faith. Therefore, it is important in determining the overall effectiveness of this discipleship program to research its impact on community bonding. Are the members actively reaching out through service projects or community outreach? Are members actively sharing their faith through witnessing? These are some of the evidence of a healthy, lively community.

Technology can play an important role in assessing any discipleship program. These will afford the opportunity for communication, progress checks, and participant feedback through online platforms and apps. The use of technology, however, has to be done wisely to ensure it enhances and does not replace personal interaction and real pastoral care. Technology can serve to facilitate communication among discipleship group members who live too far apart to easily communicate in other ways. It may provide tools to track progress or organize events. The human element always should be the most important one.

Prayer and deep dependence on the Holy Spirit need to lead and undergird the entire evaluation process. In seeking to interpret data for true insight regarding the real outcomes of the discipleship programs, may God give us wisdom and discernment. We want our evaluations to be less about quantifying success and more about discerning the work of God in individual and community lives. It is crucial to be humble and recognize that the final measure of success does not lie in our efforts but in God's grace and power. We need to be constantly looking to the Holy Spirit for guidance and direction as we assess our discipleship and spiritual formation programs.

The evaluation of discipleship and spiritual formation must be holistic and multi-dimensional. It goes beyond mere numerical measurements to incorporate qualitative data, observation, and a focus on integrating faith in life. Intentional program design, regular feedback mechanisms, and dependence on God's guidance all work together to accurately measure our efforts' effectiveness in celebrating genuine spiritual growth and strengthening in Christ. Success will be measured not in the numbers but in the transformed lives, living their faith in the world around them authentically. All marketing by the church should not be looked at in a vacuum but as part of this whole approach to spiritual development. Make sure our strategies for outreach support and enhance the spiritual growth of individuals in our community.

Celebrating Successes and Learning from Challenges

Building on the holistic evaluation discussed in the last chapter, we move into probably the most important element: reviewing past outreach efforts. This is not an exercise in self-congratulation or self-flagellation but a vital process of learning, growth, and refinement necessary to align our church's marketing with God's plan. It is about testing what works, what does not, and why. Self-awareness and humility are often in short supply in today's busy, achievement-oriented culture. We must be willing to look at our successes and failures alike, seeking God's wisdom to discern the lessons He has embedded within each.

Let's start by celebrating our successes. What initiatives really connected with the community? Which outreach programs saw heavy participation and, more importantly, measurable spiritual growth among those who attended? Perhaps a certain social media campaign surprisingly led to some deep conversations about faith. Or perhaps a community event gave rise to real relationships and resulted in the addition of many new people into the church family. Recording instances of success for encouragement and identifying the reasons behind their successes is important. Were they the result of a clear expression of our church's mission? Were they planned with creativity in terms of ways to connect? Was it because of much prayer and reliance on God's leading? Carefully analyzing these aspects will equip us to replicate successful strategies in the future.

For example, consider a church that launched a weekly online Bible study. While initial attendance might have been modest, the consistent engagement and personal testimonies from participants might reveal a surprising depth of impact. Or, a small group ministry to a specific demographic, perhaps young adults or senior citizens, may have yielded a richer harvest of discipleship than larger, more generalized programs. These small victories are worthy of celebration and careful examination, for they provide valuable insights into effective methods of reaching specific segments of the community. Don't forget the anecdotal evidence: stories of transformation, accounts of lives changed, and the testimonies of those who found faith and community through your church's efforts. These stories are at the heart of our ministry success and provide compelling evidence that our efforts bear fruit.

Of course, celebrating successes shouldn't blind us to the need for equally honest reflection on what didn't go so well. What outreach initiatives fell flat? Why were they unsuccessful in drawing participation or effecting the desired spiritual growth? Was the message unclear or poorly communicated? Did the format of the program not resonate with the target audience? Was there a lack of promotion or engagement? Or was the timing wrong, or the platform impractical for our intended demographic? While such failures may be disappointing, they are also invaluable opportunities for learning and growth. They offer an opportunity to sharpen our methods, realign our direction, and enhance the success of our future outreach.

Imagine a church that heavily invested in a large-scale community event only to be met with low attendance. Instead of merely writing off this effort as a failure, close examination may show numerous contributing factors. Was the event properly advertised? Was the date conflicting with other events in the community? Was the event itself engaging and appealing to the target audience? Was the location accessible and convenient? Analyzing these elements will help the church draw on the experience and execute more successful events in the future. Equally, a social media campaign could have few meaningful interactions. It does not necessarily reflect on the message itself but perhaps in targeted outreach, ineffective strategy of communication, or engagement with followers. These weaknesses put us in a position to make changes and thus create more effective campaigns in the future that can reach our target audience and bring them into spiritual growth.

This review process is not just about finding out mistakes but to find out the whys of success and failures. What underlying principles contributed to effective outreach? What obstacles hindered our efforts? Were there unforeseen circumstances? Was there a lack of prayer or reliance on God's guidance? This deeper level of analysis is crucial for future planning and helps us to ensure that our marketing efforts align with our mission and values. As this is worked out in personal, prayerful, and conscientious obedience to God's leading, we'll find patterns to refine over time. By doing this, we'll begin to see the different needs that are out in our community and work at developing better outreach strategies that will effectively meet those specific needs. This takes participation at multiple levels by people at your church through leadership, volunteer bases, and active involvement with outreach ministries.

This is a continuous process of review and refinement. It's not a point-in-time exercise, but a process of continuous evaluation, adaptation, and improvement. There is learning from both successes and failures, and there is realization that even the best-intentioned initiatives will not always succeed consistently. The important thing is not to be discouraged by the failures but to embrace them as learning opportunities. We must take these lessons and use them to refine our methods, renewing our commitment to the faithful sharing of the Gospel. Through this ongoing cycle of reflection and refinement, guided by the Holy Spirit, we can incrementally enhance the effectiveness of our church's outreach, ensuring our efforts accurately reflect God's love and reach the hearts and minds of those in our community and beyond. Our marketing strategies remain relevant and practical in this continuous improvement, hence glorifying God. It is not just about increasing attendance or social media engagement but about people's spiritual development and deepening our community's connection with Christ.

This holistic view of success requires embracing ongoing evaluation, learning from successes and challenges, and submitting God's guidance at every outreach step. By adopting this continuous cycle of assessment and refinement, we can ensure that our church's marketing efforts attract people to Christ, nurture their faith, and equip them to live authentically in the world.

Ultimately, the accurate measure of our success is not in numbers but in transformed lives living out their faith authentically, a testament to the transformative power of Christ's love working within and through us. Our efforts should be a strong, vibrant, and loving community in Christ and His teachings, which epitomize the essence of God's love. By continuously learning, adapting, and seeking God's guidance, our church's marketing can become a powerful instrument for spreading the Gospel and impacting the world. Let's continually seek God's guidance, asking for wisdom, discernment, and the strength to serve His purposes faithfully.

Chapter 10

Next Steps and Continued Growth

Reflecting on Current Outreach Strategies

Before launching into new ventures, it is essential to take a close look at what your church is already doing in the way of outreach. This is not an exercise in self-criticism but rather one in which you discern what is working, what isn't, and where God may be leading your church next. It's a reflective process-prayerful, honest, and with a cross-section of your ministry's key leaders and team members.

Start by gathering information. What are you currently doing to reach your community? This might include your website, social media presence, email newsletters, printed materials, community events, partnerships with local organizations, and even word-of-mouth referrals. For each, gather specific statistics: How many visitors to your website each month? How is the social media interaction? How many come to your events? What does the community say? Don't just focus on numbers but also on qualitative data like testimonials, comments, and observations from your team. What stories are emerging from your current outreach?

Once you've collected your data, analyze its effectiveness in light of your church's mission and vision. Are your current strategies truly reflecting your core values and beliefs? Are they effectively communicating your unique message to your target audience? Are they producing the spiritual fruit you're looking for-conversions, maturing Christians, and a growing body of believers? If not, why not? What are the challenges that you're facing? Are there internal obstacles, such as resistance to change or resource shortages, or is something external impeding your progress?

Look at all the dimensions of your outreach. If you use social media, evaluate your content strategy. Is it engaging, authentic, and reflective of God's love? Are you actively listening to your audience and responding to their needs and questions? Are you sharing diverse content, including stories, testimonials, and practical resources? If your church uses email marketing, review your email campaigns. Are they clear, concise, and relevant to your audience? Are you providing value, promoting upcoming events, and building community? Are your open and click-through rates positive, and what does this say to you about reader engagement?

Look at your website. Is it user-friendly and attractive? Is it easy to navigate? Does it effectively communicate the mission, values, and community of your church? Is it mobile-friendly? Are service times, location, and contact information easy to find? Does it provide ways to engage, like online giving, event registration, or to sign up to volunteer? You may want to examine analytics to see what part of your website is working and what is not.

If there are regular community events for your church, evaluate those. How well were they attended? Was your message conveyed with the event? Did it facilitate connecting and building relationships in a meaningful way? What did the people say about their experience? Were there any logistical problems that need to be worked out for future events? Evaluate your strategy regarding partnerships with other local organizations. Are they mutually beneficial, in which you can serve the community while increasing your reach? Do your partnerships make good use of shared resources, promoting mutual growth and development?

Beyond the specific means, consider your general philosophy of outreach. Is there a consistent vision and plan directing your work? Is your vision understood and bought into by all your team members? Is communication and collaboration clear among your team members? Are you measuring the success of your outreach, not just in numbers, but in spiritual growth and community impact? Are your metrics aligned with your overall mission and vision, or do you find yourselves focusing on vanity metrics rather than those that indicate true spiritual impact?

This reflective process is not just about looking at the past performance. It's about learning from your experiences, finding areas for improvement, and coming up with a refined vision for the future. It's a crucial step toward creating a more effective and impactful outreach plan that reflects God's love and glorifies His name. Remember that this assessment isn't simply a solo activity but a collaborative effort involving key stakeholders within your church. Their insights and perspectives are essential for creating a comprehensive and well-rounded picture of your current outreach strategies. Encourage open communication and value diverse viewpoints.

Consider using a SWOT analysis: Strengths, Weaknesses, Opportunities, and Threats to frame this reflective process. Identify your church's strengths in outreach-a strong volunteer base, a vibrant social media presence, and effective community partnerships. Then, acknowledge weaknesses: low website traffic, limited resources, and lack of diversity in your outreach methods. Identify growth opportunities: unexplored demographics within your community, potential new partnerships, and emerging digital tools. Finally, consider any threats that might impede your outreach efforts: competition from other churches, negative community perceptions, and changes in the technological landscape. This self-evaluation aims not to point out mistakes but to provide a fuller understanding of where you are now. An honest assessment will enable you to determine what works for you and what needs to be adjusted. This will, in turn, be used to formulate a workable plan for action in the future.

Through this, your resources shall become well utilized, and your efforts will be congruent with the general mission statement your church has adopted. Thus, this reflective process may enable you to refine current practices and confidently press forward into new initiatives, led by God's great grace and inspired by His never-failing love. Remember to embrace successes and failures as valuable learning experiences and approach this assessment with prayerful humility, seeking God's guidance at every step. Through this careful reflection, you'll be better equipped to create a genuinely impactful outreach strategy that transforms lives and expands God's kingdom.

Developing an Actionable Plan for the Future

Building on the self-assessment regarding your church's current strategies for outreach, the following essential process is the concrete and operational plan toward your future. This will be a prayer-led, fluid action plan, not an unchangeable document of rules to hamstring your work in an ever-changing ministry environment. A living document, the outreach plan will be continuously scrutinized and adapted as needed during your growth process. The key is setting clear goals, defining the strategies, allocating resources to support them, and setting measurable outcomes within your church context and God's leading.

Start by identifying global objectives. What do you want to accomplish in the next year, three or five years? These should be parallel to your church's mission statement and reflect what you understand God's call on your community to be. Are you trying to increase attendance? Reach a certain demographic? Deepen the discipleship of your current members? Expand your community outreach? Be concrete and measurable whenever you can. Instead of simply trying to achieve "more community involvement," define a concrete, measurable goal, such as "increase volunteer involvement in community service projects by 25% over the next year."

After you have defined your goals, create concrete ways to achieve them. That is where the concepts throughout this book come in. Take, for example, different outreach methods: social media engagement, targeted advertising, community events, partnerships with local organizations, small group ministries, personal evangelism training, or even the use of new technologies for online worship and connection. For each of these strategies, list specific actions to be taken. For instance, your strategy for increasing social media engagement might include creating a content calendar, scheduling regular posts, engaging with followers, and running paid advertising. In developing each strategy, create an action plan that describes who is responsible, when the action needs to be completed, and what resources are needed.

Resource allocation should be effective. Determine what resources are available to your church: financial, human, and technological. Evaluate carefully how these resources can best support your chosen strategies. Prioritize initiatives that align most closely with your goals and have the most significant potential for impact. Your resources are precious gifts from God; wise stewardship is a necessary part of responsible ministry. Don't try to do too many things; focus your resources on those initiatives that demonstrate the greatest promise. This may require saying "no" to some opportunities to say "yes" to others that more effectively serve God's purposes.

Crucially, establish methods for measuring your progress. While the ultimate measure of success is transforming lives and strengthening faith, having quantifiable metrics helps to track your progress and identify areas needing adjustment. These might include website traffic, social media engagement, event attendance, volunteer participation, or the number of people who have responded to an invitation to connect with your church. Review these metrics regularly to assess the effectiveness of your strategies and make adjustments as needed. And remember flexibility is crucial. What works well in one season may not work quite as well in another. Be prepared to adjust your strategy based on your analysis of the outcome.

Beyond the measurable, don't forget the qualitative assessment. This means intentionally soliciting responses from your congregation, visitors, and community partners. Conduct surveys, interviews, or focus groups to assess the effectiveness of your outreach efforts. Are people finding your messages relevant and engaging? Are your events well-attended and impactful? Is the love of Christ flowing through you to people? This qualitative data brings out valuable information that would otherwise not be captured in the quantitative data. You begin to understand whether your attempts are working, how they work, and if you really reach people's hearts.

To that end, make a powerful prayer life part of developing your plan of action. Start every planning session in prayer, asking God for wisdom and guidance in all the decisions made. Regularly lead your church leadership and team members in prayer for God's blessing in this effort and His discernment in navigating the challenge. Remember, this is a plan, not a sign of human ingenuity but of partnering with God as He advances His kingdom. And it is your dependent prayer for His guidance that forms your actions and ensures, really, that your marketing is a reflection of His love and grace.

Once the plan is there, execute it consistently. Establish clear communication channels, informing everyone of the progress and challenges, and the changes affected. Regularly review the plan for revision with feedback and results. Let the plan be a living document that grows along with your ministry. The ultimate success of your church marketing efforts isn't in numbers or in metrics; it's in the transformative power of the Gospel to change lives. Your focus should be sharing the love of Christ in natural and relevant ways. Make sure your plan is in line with your church's mission statement and unique needs and contexts of your community. Think about demographics, cultural norms, and social issues affecting your community. Adapt your strategies to touch the real needs and concerns of those you're trying to reach. Knowing your community is the most important thing in outreach.

Celebrate your successes! Acknowledge and appreciate your team's contributions and God's blessings. Recognizing and celebrating successes boosts morale and motivates your team to continue working toward your shared goals. Regular celebrations, even small ones, strengthen team unity and reinforce the positive impact of your collective work.

The development of a successful outreach plan is an ongoing process. It's not an event but a cycle of planning, implementation, evaluation, and refinement. Be patient, persistent, and prayerful. Trust God to bless your efforts as you consistently apply these principles, guiding your church toward continued growth and fruitful ministry. The journey may be challenging at times, but the reward of sharing the love of Christ and building His kingdom is immeasurable.

Seeking Accountability and Support

As we've explored, effective church marketing is not a solitary journey. While prayer and reliance on God's guidance are paramount, the process is significantly enhanced through the support and accountability of others. This isn't simply about sharing successes; it's about navigating challenges, receiving wise counsel, and consistently focusing on the goal: glorifying God and expanding His kingdom. Next, it will be important to identify those individuals or groups who can provide this critical support for your continued development. Consider first your current leadership structure. Are there those in your church who already possess a solid understanding of marketing principles or demonstrate a natural instinct regarding strategic planning and outreach? These would be great mentors and sounding boards. Maybe someone on your church council, a committed volunteer, or even a pastor with marketing experience can lend a keen eye and offer advice. Do not be afraid to reach out to them and have an open conversation about your needs. Describe your vision for future outreach and invite them to be a part of the development and delivery of the plan.

Outside of the current leadership structure, extend your network. Networking isn't about self-promotion; it's about building relationships and seeking wisdom from others walking a similar path. Are there other churches in your community or denomination with successful outreach programs? Reach out to their leadership to not copy their strategies but learn from their experience. Go to conferences and workshops on church marketing and ministry. These events offer a very real opportunity to interact with fellow leaders, share ideas, and get new insights.

Accountability: It does little good to plan in the most meticulous way if, without it, the plans fail in application. Determine someone who will hold you accountable- just a few trusted confidants will be great to encourage honest, healthy, constructive criticism. An accountability partner is more than a buddy that will celebrate success and honestly advise you in case some issues crop up. This could be a fellow pastor, a trusted elder, a member of your church staff, or a trusted friend from outside of your church. What is important is that you find someone whose judgment you respect and whose opinion you value, and who is committed to prayerfully supporting your efforts.

It is important that you have regular meetings with your accountability partner(s). These gatherings need to be more than a simple update on status; it's time for honest reflection, prayer, and strategic planning. During this meeting, discuss how it's going toward your goals, where roadblocks may be, and brainstorm creative solutions. Take this opportunity to learn from mistakes, readjust your approach, and seek guidance in prayer. The frequency of these will, of course, depend upon the complexity of your outreach plan and the needs within your church. However, regular interaction—perhaps monthly or even bi-weekly—ensures ongoing support and guidance.

Besides that, formal mentorship programs can be hugely helpful. Many denominations and church organizations offer formal mentorship programs to help church leaders with a variety of facets of ministry, including how to market and reach their communities. Such a program affords you the opportunity to interact with highly experienced mentors who will be able to offer personalized advice and support based on your needs and situation. Such mentors often have years of experience in navigating the challenges of church marketing, thus providing insights that could save you considerable time and effort.

In addition to formal mentorship, consider forming a specific outreach and marketing committee or team. This will give the leadership a place to brainstorm ideas together, plan events, and put them into action. The team should be composed of diverse perspectives and talents within your church, providing creativity and synergy toward your outreach effort. It will need to meet on a regular basis, and each member's role should be well-defined with uniform goals.

Besides human accountability, remember spiritual accountability. The prayer and seeking God's guidance in all areas of your outreach plan are not to be compromised. Make no major decisions without first taking time to pray over it. Pray for God's wisdom in selecting marketing strategies, in the resourcing, and in measuring the outcome. Spiritual disciplines such as fasting and Bible study can further strengthen your spiritual foundation and sharpen your discernment in navigating the complexities of church marketing.

It will not work any better than your willingness to be open and honest. Both your successes and failures should be shared with your accountability partners. Don't be afraid to admit when you make a mistake or to ask for help when you need it. Remember, leadership and vulnerability go hand in glove; it builds trust and opens doors to growth and learning. You create a safer space for feedback and support by building a culture of transparency.

Remember, too, that accountability isn't just about correcting errors; it's also about celebrating successes. When you achieve a milestone or see evidence of God's work through your outreach efforts, share that with your accountability partners. Celebrating wins together not only builds morale but reinforces the importance of your collective efforts. Acknowledging the struggles and the victories fosters a sense of shared purpose, strengthening your commitment to your collective mission.

An accountability system shouldn't be static; it's supposed to grow with your church and your outreach projects. Check regularly if the accountability structure is working for you; adjust where necessary. Are you receiving the support and feedback that you need? Are your accountability partners providing the critique and encouragement? Through regular assessment, you can continue to refine and improve the accountability structure over time.

The resources available to support your efforts extend beyond individuals. Consider utilizing online forums and communities dedicated to church marketing and ministry. These platforms provide access to other church leaders' information, resources, and advice. Engaging in these online communities provides opportunities for collaboration, networking, and learning from shared experiences.

Many denominations and ministries are committed to equipping the local church with training and resources to develop effective outreach programs. These may prove invaluable in providing additional tools and strategies to help improve your marketing efforts. Check with your denomination, local church networks, or national Christian organizations to see what's available. These resources can better prepare you to reach your community and spread the Good News of Jesus Christ.

To God you are ultimately responsible. While human accountability is important, it's very important to keep God's will in the clear light and seek His guidance on every aspect of your ministry. The effectiveness of your outreach should be determined by how it touches lives and draws people closer to God. Thus, prayer, self-reflection, and keeping spiritual principles in constant focus are at the core of a successful church marketing strategy. Combining human support with spiritual accountability sets a good platform for further growth and a fruitful ministry.

Embracing Continuous Learning and Adaptation

The digital age brings about unprecedented opportunities and significant challenges in regard to church outreach. Even methods that worked effectively five years ago may be considered outdated or ineffective today. Continuous learning and adaptation are therefore not only beneficial but an absolute necessity in order to be relevant and reach an even broader audience with the Gospel. It is not about trend chasing for the sake of it but finding effective ways using whatever tools one has at their disposal to meet the people where they are. Take social media platforms: what started out as one-stop shopping with

Facebook now shows a base migration with a younger demographic starting to switch to other channels such as Instagram, TikTok, and YouTube. To effectively reach younger generations, a church has to understand these platforms, their nuances, and the best ways to engage users in a real and respectful manner. This commitment to learning and growing doesn't stop with the latest social media trends; it's about understanding the deeper cultural landscape and evolving needs of the community you're called to serve. Demographic changes, economic shifts, and changing social ills all influence how people interact with religion and religious bodies. Informed through research, community engagement, and one-on-one conversations with your congregation, this is critical for determining how to adapt your outreach. Study community demographics on a regular basis. What are the missing age brackets within your congregation? What do they enjoy? Where do they spend their time online and offline? Understanding this will really help you in the development of more targeted and effective outreach strategies.

Active participation in conferences, workshops, and seminars is another important aspect of continuous learning. These events provide opportunities to learn from experienced church leaders, marketing professionals, and other experts in the field. Look for events that specifically focus on digital marketing for churches, social media strategies for faith-based organizations, and best practices in community engagement. Equally important is networking with other attendees, sharing experiences, learning from each other's successes and challenges, and building relationships that can provide ongoing support and guidance.

Beyond formal training, informal learning is equally important. Engage in continuous self-directed learning through reading of books, articles, and blogs on church marketing, digital outreach, and community engagement. Subscribe to various related newsletters and podcasts to stay up-to-date with current issues and best practices in these fields. Follow influential church leaders, marketing experts, and organizations on social media platforms to learn from their various strategies and approaches. Gain new information and perspectives to refine constantly your understanding of effective church outreach. Never be afraid to try new things, but always ground your efforts in prayer and discernment.

Continuous learning is not only about the acquisition of new skills and knowledge but also about adjusting strategies in response to feedback and results. It means being flexible, changing course when necessary, and learning from successes and failures. Assess regularly the effectiveness of outreach efforts with appropriate metrics. While the focus remains on spiritual growth and transformed lives, data can provide valuable insights into what resonates with your target audience and what needs improvement. This could involve analyzing website traffic, social media engagement, event attendance, and feedback from surveys or personal interactions.

Regularly review your website analytics. What pages are most popular? Which ones receive the least traffic? This will help you understand what works for your audience and what doesn't. If you're using social media, track your engagement metrics. How many people are engaging with your posts? What types of content are getting the most engagement? These metrics can help you further refine your content strategy and effectively target your efforts. Equally important is conducting surveys and gathering feedback from your congregation. Ask members what they find helpful, what could be improved, and what topics they want addressed. This direct input can go a long way in improving your outreach strategies and serving your community's needs.

Feedback shouldn't be thought of as merely a method of measuring success. It's actually a gateway to further growth and refinement. Negative feedback is often hard to swallow but is worth its weight in gold regarding finding the areas that need improvement. It allows for much-needed reflection and course correction to keep your outreach at its most efficient and meaningful. Create an environment where your church leadership is free with openness and transparency; constructive criticism, if approached as a necessary step of growth, is welcomed and shared naturally. Set up systems whereby feedback is constantly solicited through formal surveys, personal discussions, or online feedback mechanisms.

Adaptability also calls for flexibility in letting go of strategies that are failing. Just because something was successful earlier doesn't necessarily mean that it will also be as effective in the future. Be willing to experiment with different strategies, and equally let go of what is not working. That requires a bit of humility, being able to say you don't have the answers, and you are going to learn from your mistakes. There should be an easy, set way to assess your marketing efforts and make changes, always referring back to the ultimate purpose that your church has for outreach.

Continuous learning and adaptation are ongoing processes. It's not an event; it is a commitment to lifelong growth and improvement. Foster an attitude of learning within your church by encouraging staff and volunteers to pursue knowledge and skills consistently. This makes the church dynamic and adaptive, ever in the quest to serve the community better, as well as share the message of Christ in ways most effective. Keep learning, keep involved, and never stop growing.

Communications are constantly changing; one must be flexible and adapt to them. By putting a high value on continuous learning and adapting, you set your church up for continued growth and an Impact that lasts in the lives of those you serve. Keep in mind that all of your outreach efforts are to bring people to God and to establish a strong, active community of faith, love, and service.

Trusting in God's Guidance and Provision

After working through the details of modern church marketing, embracing innovation, and clinging to our faith, we find ourselves now at a point where a decision needs to be made: to trust God's leading and provisioning for the next steps. This is not about a project being concluded; rather, it's a continuous process of faith, a cocreating with the Divine, extending His kingdom. The strategies discussed-from leveraging digital platforms to fostering genuine community engagement-are tools and instruments in the hands of God's servants. Their effectiveness depends not solely on our skill and diligence but profoundly on our reliance on His grace and wisdom.

Our previous discussions highlighted the necessity of adapting to the evolving digital landscape. This adaptation, however, should never take precedence over our primary objective: to honor God and represent the Gospel in an authentic way. Our metrics must support this principle. As good as website traffic, social media hits, and physical attendance may be, the bottom line in measuring success will always be changed lives, strengthened faith, and a community founded on Christ's love. We need to keep asking ourselves one thing: Are we drawing people closer to God? Are we making a more loving community stronger? Are we forming disciples that will make other disciples?

It requires a fresh way of looking. We are not just managing a marketing campaign but shepherding souls. Our strategies are to be more than techniques -they are ways of expression for our faith. By its very nature, our approach must be humble with acknowledgment of our inadequacies and dependence upon the power of God alone. Prayer becomes not merely a pre-campaign ritual but more of a constant companion along the way. In prayer lies clarity, guidance, and the strength to press through challenges. Prayer provides the lifeblood for effective and God-honoring marketing. This is where creativity, persistence, and discernment for God's will regarding your ministry come from.

Think of all the examples in Scripture of God's people who, facing insurmountable obstacles, triumphed through faith and prayer. Moses led the Israelites out of slavery, not by an army, but by obedience to God's commands and constant prayer. David, as a young shepherd boy, slew Goliath, not because his weapons were superior, but because he had confidence in God's power. These stories remind one poignantly that God's strength is made perfect in our weakness. When the challenges of church outreach overwhelm us and we question whether we will ever reach an indifferent world, we must remember God is with us, ordering our steps, and supplying our needs.

This trust in God's provision extends to practical matters. Funding, resources, and exemplary volunteers are gifts from God, given to us in His perfect timing. When resources are scarce, instead of panicking or compromising our integrity, we should seek God's wisdom as to how to manage our resources, trusting in His provision. He often works in unexpected ways, opening doors we never anticipated and providing solutions we could not have foreseen. We are to be good stewards of what He has provided, managing our resources wisely and seeking His direction in their use through prayer.

This trust requires sometimes stepping out in faith, sight unseen. God asks us a lot of impossible things often, which reach beyond comfort zones and call us entirely to lean upon Him. This takes courage, persistence, and openness to the unknown. It is at those times of uncertainty that our faith will be tested and, ironically, it is where it will be strengthened. Just think of Abraham being asked to sacrifice his son Isaac: an incomprehensible request, and yet, by obedience, Abraham demonstrated a complete trust in God's plan. Small acts of faith can be as powerful a testament to devotion as grand ones are.

Nurturing within the church an atmosphere of trust and reliance on God is important. This involves openness in communication, mutual support, and a shared understanding of our dependence on the Holy Spirit. Team meetings should become opportunities for prayer, seeking God's guidance in decision-making, and celebrating His blessings. Volunteers should be empowered to share their gifts and talents, trusting that God will use them to further His kingdom. Leaders should model humility and vulnerability, acknowledging their limitations and seeking the wisdom of others. In this way, mutual trust and reliance on God create a strong, cohesive community that can overcome any obstacle.

Yes, the challenges of church marketing are real, but so is the power of God. He has equipped us with everything we need to succeed-not by strength, but by His grace. As we forge ahead, remember that learning is always ongoing, adaptation is part of the process, and faith is always unshakeable. Let us position our strategies according to the Word of God, guide every decision by

His leading, and trust in His provision for all our needs. May our marketing not simply be about the means to an end, but a reflection of God's love and a signpost in these dark times that a world searching is trying to find truth.

Faith Is Not Is easy, it Is often characterized with challenges, setbacks, and periods of doubt. Rather, it is in times like these that our confidence in God gets refined and deepened. The path ahead may be uncertain, but our destination is secure. With God as our guide, we can confidently face any obstacle, knowing His love, grace, and provision are sure. Our focus should not be on the immediate results but on our unwavering commitment to serve God and His people. Let us strive to be faithful and diligent and trust in the one who holds the future in His hands.

The importance of celebrating victories, large and small. These are not just times of self-congratulation but times of thanking God for His blessings and encouraging one another in our common ministry. Every soul that comes to Christ, every life transformed, every community strengthened-are all victories to be celebrated, testaments to the power of God's work through our efforts.

As we conclude this exploration of God's outreach plan, let us reflect on the profound privilege we have been given: to be instruments in God's hands, sharing His love and grace with a world in desperate need. Our work is not about personal achievement but about fulfilling God's purpose. Let us approach our tasks humbly, recognizing that God works through us, not our capabilities. This realization will bring about deeper appreciation and reliance on Him, yielding a more efficient and meaningful ministry.

May the grace of our Lord Jesus Christ, the love of God, and the fellowship of the Holy Spirit be with us always as we keep proclaiming the good news of the Gospel and building up His kingdom here on earth. Let us pray for wisdom, guidance, and strength to continue this vital work, and always remember that our true success is measured not in numbers or metrics but in lives changed and hearts transformed by the power of God's love. The journey is ongoing, and the grace of God is sufficient for every step of the way. Let us trust in Him completely.

Acknowledgments

First and foremost, I offer my deepest gratitude to God, the source of all wisdom and inspiration. This book would not have been possible without His guidance and unwavering support. I am also profoundly thankful to my family for their patience, understanding, and constant encouragement throughout the writing process. Their love and support have been instrumental in bringing this project to fruition.

I sincerely appreciate Pastor Jerry G., church leaders, and marketing professionals who generously shared their time, insights, and experiences. Their contributions have enriched this book immeasurably and provided valuable real-world examples that bring the concepts to life. I am incredibly grateful to the President of Newburgh Seminary and President Mollett specifically for their invaluable contributions and support.

Appendix

A. Resources for Effective Church Outreach

1. Recommended Books and Articles

- *The Purpose Driven Church* by Rick Warren
- *Marketing for Congregations: Choosing to Succeed* by Norman Shaw Chuck and Philip Kotler
- *Outreach and Evangelism Handbook* by Thomas Rainer

2. Websites and Online Tools

- Canva: For creating church marketing materials.
- Unsplashed: Free high-quality images for church projects.
- Buffer: Social media scheduling tool for consistent outreach.

3. Software for Church Management

- Planning Center: Comprehensive church management software.
- Faithlife: Church-focused tools for digital engagement.

B. Practical Templates and Checklists

1. Church Event Marketing Checklist

- Define event goals and target audience.
- Develop a promotional timeline.
- Create marketing materials (flyers, social media posts, emails).
- Use local partnerships for broader outreach.
- Evaluate event success post-completion.

2. Social Media Post Template

o   Opening: Start with an engaging question or Bible verse.

o   Body: Share key details of your message or event.

o   Closing: Include a call-to-action

C. Biblical References for Outreach Inspiration

1. *The Great Commission*: Matthew 28:18-20

2. *Salt and Light*: Matthew 5:13-16

3. *The Parable of the Sower*: Matthew 13:1-23

4. *The Acts of the Apostles*: Acts 2:42-47, focusing on community and growth.

D. Reflection Questions for Church Leaders

1. How does our outreach strategy reflect God's character and love?

2. What are the primary needs of our community, and how can we address them?

3. Can we effectively use digital and traditional methods to reach diverse demographics?

4. How can we measure spiritual transformation beyond numerical growth?

E. Sample Surveys for Community Feedback

1. **Post-Service Feedback Form**

    o   Was today's message relatable and impactful?

    o   Are there areas where the church can improve its support or services?

2. **Community Needs Survey**

    o   What are the most pressing issues in our neighborhood?

    o   What types of programs or services would you find valuable?

Glossary

Authenticity: In the context of church marketing, this refers to genuine and transparent communication that reflects the church's values and beliefs.

Community Engagement: Building relationships and connecting with individuals and organizations within the church's local community.

Conversion Rate: The percentage of individuals who take a desired action, such as attending a church service or signing up for a program, after exposure to a marketing effort. While necessary, this should not be the sole measure of success.

Discipleship: The process of guiding and mentoring individuals in their spiritual growth and development.

Engagement (Digital): Users' interaction and involvement with online church content.

Evangelization: The act of sharing the Gospel message and making disciples.

Faith-Based Marketing: Marketing strategies grounded in Christian values and principles prioritize authentic connection and spiritual transformation over numerical results.

Outreach: Initiatives and strategies employed by churches to share the Gospel and connect with people in their communities.

Spiritual Transformation: The process of individuals experiencing a profound change in their lives due to encountering Christ.

References

Books and Publications

1. Barna Group. *The State of the Church: Insights and Trends from Modern Christianity*. Ventura, CA: Barna Research, 2019.

2. Kotler, Philip, and Norman Shawchuck. *Marketing for Congregations: Choosing to Succeed*. Nashville, TN: Abingdon Press, 1992.

3. Malphurs, Aubrey. *The Nuts and Bolts of Church Planting: A Guide for Starting Any Church*. Grand Rapids, MI: Baker Books, 2011.

4. Rainer, Thom S. *The Unchurched Next Door: Understanding Faith Stages as Keys to Sharing Your Faith*. Grand Rapids, MI: Zondervan, 2003.

5. Warren, Rick. *The Purpose Driven Church: Growth Without Compromising Your Message and Mission*. Grand Rapids, MI: Zondervan, 1995.

Biblical Sources

1. The Holy Bible, New International Version. Biblica, Inc.

2. Matthew 28:18–20 (*The Great Commission*).

3. Acts 2:42–47 (*The Acts of the Apostles*).

4. Matthew 13:1–23 (*The Parable of the Sower*).

5. Matthew 5:13–16 (*Salt and Light*).

Online Resources

1. Barna Group. "Research and Trends for Church Growth." www.barna.com.

2. Unsplashed. "Free High-Quality Images for Church Marketing." www.unsplash.com.

3. Canva. "Create Beautiful Graphics for Your Church." www.canva.com.

4. Buffer. "Social Media Management for Churches." www.buffer.com.

Research and Case Studies

1. Pew Research Center. *Religion and Public Life: Trends in Church Attendance and Engagement.* www.pewforum.org, 2022.

2. Lifeway Research. *Engaging the Unchurched: Practical Insights for Church Growth.* Nashville, TN: Lifeway, 2020.

3. Christianity Today. *Digital Outreach: The Role of Social Media in Modern Evangelism.* www.christianitytoday.com.

Other Resources

1. Faith life. "Tools and Resources for Church Engagement." www.faithlife.com.

2. Planning Center. "Comprehensive Church Management Software." www.planningcenter.com.

Author Biography

I am Dr. Manfred Gobai, Ph. D., a Christian author passionate about inspiring personal growth and economic wisdom through faith-based storytelling. I hold a B.A. in Christian Education, an M.A., and a Ph.D. in Christian Sales and Marketing from Newburgh Theology Seminary and Bible College.

As a financial expert and storyteller, I bring a unique blend of practical experience and spiritual insight to my work, with a particular focus on economic freedom and justice. Having spent years navigating the stock market and exploring faith-based financial strategies, I aim to empower individuals to live purposefully and generously. My writing, including **"God's Outreach Plan:Marketing the Church in Modern Times"** reflects my deep commitment to helping people understand the intersection of faith, freedom, and finance.

I am dedicated to sharing messages of hope, financial responsibility, and spiritual empowerment through my work. By integrating faith and wisdom into our economic decisions, we can achieve personal liberation and contribute to justice and equity in our communities. I aim to inspire others to embrace purposeful living and see faith's transformative power in every aspect of life.